HEALING AMERICAN DEMOCRACY:
GOING LOCAL

MIKE HAIS, DOUG ROSS
AND MORLEY WINOGRAD

BLUE ZEPHYR

SAN FRANCISCO

Published by Blue Zephyr

Copyright © 2018 by Mike and Morley, LLC

www.golocal.us.com

ISBN-13: 978-1985888401
ISBN-10: 1985888408

Healing American Democracy:
Going Local

Mike Hais, Doug Ross, and Morley Winograd

"If there are any ills that democracy is suffering from today,
they can only be cured by more democracy."
-- New York Governor, Al Smith, 1923

PRAISE FOR *HEALING AMERICAN DEMOCRACY*

"Messrs Hais, Ross, and Winograd have stumbled upon a simple yet brilliant idea for how to fix American democracy: empower localities to create their own political and civic solutions while using the Constitution as the bedrock for civil rights. From Kalamazoo to Denver, and Knoxville to New Orleans, they provide stories about local success, places where leaders have responded to their constituents' needs in a way the federal government never could and rebuilt civic trust in the process. The authors' optimism and creativity have been sorely needed and should be welcomed by those on both the left and the right. On one thing all Americans should be able to agree - we need new solutions and this book offers many that are worthy."

Michael Smerconish, SiriusXM, CNN, and Sunday Philadelphia Inquirer.

"Here's a brilliant, alternative solution to our national woes. The notion of bringing power back to communities represents the potential upside in an information age that, to date, has driven greater centralization, economic concentration and horrendous levels of polarization. This should be a foundational text, not to any one political perspective, but to the entire polity."

Joel Kotkin, Presidential Fellow in Urban Futures, Chapman University and Executive Director, Center for Opportunity Urbanism

"Tip O'Neill said 'All politics is local.' As Mike Hais, Doug Ross, and Morley Winograd explore in this valuable work, while Washington is riven by polarization, some of the most innovative and important policies are flowing from local communities today."

David Axelrod, Founder and Director of the University of Chicago Institute of Politics

"*Healing American Democracy: Going Local,* is a welcome antidote to the Trump era. Citizens who can't bring themselves to stop watching the train wreck that is Washington D.C. should take a break and read the argument this book makes for Constitutional Localism. It is consistent with long standing American values of self-reliance, it accommodates diversity without creating division and the focus on problem solving is in keeping with the outlook of a new and powerful generation. It is a ray of sunshine in an otherwise dismal political world."

Elaine C. Kamarck, Senior Fellow & Director, Center for Effective Public Management, Brookings Institution

"The national consensus that reigned from the New Deal through Lyndon Johnson's Great Society—that we should look to the federal government to solve our biggest problems—has unraveled. In this short book the authors explain why, then propose a replacement: that we should rely instead on local communities and regions to address most issues, within limits guaranteed by constitutional rights. This is a profound insight. Let us hope it receives a wide reading and provokes equally profound discussion about our future as a nation."

David Osborne, Progressive Policy Institute

"In this timely new work, Hais, Ross and Winograd offer a provocative antidote for what ails America. Their ideas go well beyond the overly simplistic "come together" call. Instead, they offer tangible, compelling ideas worthy of consideration by anyone who cares about democracy."

Alicia Menendez, Contributing Editor @Bustle and TV Journalist

This book is dedicated to the founders of the United States for their wisdom and political acumen in establishing our constitutional democracy nearly two and a half centuries ago and to the numerous citizens, both inside government and out, who have worked to preserve and perfect that remarkable experiment in the years since. May this book play its part in furthering the efforts of all those who believe in the power of democracy.

Table of Contents

CHAPTER ONE:
THE GROWING THREAT TO OUR DEMOCRACY

American democracy is straining to meet the governing demands of a nation that has lost much of its cohesion over the last eighty years. The outward symptoms of this growing mismatch between who we are as Americans and how we attempt to govern ourselves can be seen in the willingness of a growing number of Americans to entertain the possibility of short-circuiting democratic processes in order to break the deadlock in Washington, and get something done that addresses their problems. As we will document in this book, the acrimonious debate over American identity and the angry polarizing election of 2016 are just two of the latest symptoms of a country that has grown increasingly difficult to govern.

We believe the underlying cause of this democratic discontent is the diminishing effectiveness of the governing framework, or civic ethos, created by the New Deal that continues to define the parameters of public policy debates at the federal and state level. By championing a larger and more active role for the federal government to fashion broad national policies to manage the stresses of an industrializing society, the New Deal provided the country with a strong enough central government to battle both the Great Depression and World War II.

However, the New Deal civic ethos depended on a broad national consensus on purpose and political norms for its implementation. It has become increasingly ineffective, as the country has gone from relatively homogeneity to a citizenry defined more by its variety than by its sameness. Now, in another period of public dissatisfaction with the efficacy of democracy, we believe it is time for America to adopt a new civic ethos better suited to the much more variegated cultural, demographic, and economic landscape that challenges us in the first quarter of the twenty-first century.

This book represents our attempt to find a practical, non-ideological solution to what we believe is a serious threat to the nation's future—the growing failure of our current governing arrangements to respond to our citizens' needs and the doubts that failure is sowing about the effectiveness of democracy and democratic norms of behavior. In important ways, this challenge is unique. For never has the United States, or any other country for that matter, had to figure out how to create a large-scale democracy with such a multiplicity of economic arrangements, individual identities, life-style preferences, and cultural beliefs. Unless we can find better ways to ensure that our constitutional democracy serves the needs of Americans today, we run the risk of losing the idea of democracy to the forces of autocracy that are on the rise throughout the world.

A FEAR OF LOSING OUR DEMOCRACY

The three authors of this book are political practitioners, not academics. One of us was a political pollster before moving to Los Angles to do survey research for the entertainment industry, another was a state senator and U.S. Assistant Secretary of Labor, and the third was a state political party chair and White House senior policy advisor. We therefore come to this discussion with less of an eye to the theoretical and more of a focus on what can be done now, in very practical terms, to heal the American democracy we love so much. At the same time, our training and a lifetime of work compels us to be certain whatever strategies we are recommending are based on solid data and not on wishful thinking.

In this book, we present both what we believe is the clear and convincing evidence that the New Deal civic ethos is as out of date as the foundations on which it was built and a description of a replacement that we think will lead to a renewed faith in our democracy and its ability to govern successfully.

The reason for entering the debate over how best to respond to growing public dissatisfaction with the functioning of our democracy is our concern for the preservation of the values and rules that define it—individual freedom, rule of law, governmental checks and balances, protection of speech and dissent, and defined rights that protect the minority from the tyranny of the majority. We share the conviction that any abandonment of our American system of government, with its roots in the Declaration of Independence and the Constitution, would pose a grave threat to the American idea and our liberty.

Loss of public confidence in the federal government to solve, or even care about, the problems and concerns of ordinary people, has bred both a frustration and anger that has led a growing number of Americans to question whether strict adherence to our constitutional democratic processes is justified in a context of governmental deadlock and dysfunction. A recent PPRI/ Atlantic Report poll reported that "Six in ten white working-class Americans… say because things have gotten so far off track, we need a strong leader who is willing to break the rules." In the same study, 32% of white college graduates also shared that sentiment.[1]

Recent data also suggests that Millennials, the youngest and largest generation in the electorate, value democratic governance less than previous generations.[2] Most members of that generation didn't vote for President Trump, but their wild enthusiasm for Bernie Sanders in the Democratic primaries reflected their support for his argument that the system was rigged and needed a revolution to overturn it. The election of Donald Trump as President of the United States and the emotional reaction to him and his presidency provide daily evidence of the current frustration with American democracy, on both the right and the left, that is too widespread to be ignored.

Much of the national debate, especially since the last presidential election, has focused on the sharp divisions in this country that are indeed real—partisan, ethnic, religious, cultural, and economic. These differences are seen as pulling the country apart, and make finding consensus on nearly any thing important at the federal level difficult, if not impossible.

Pundits and politicians call for leadership that "brings us together" as the antidote to this growing divisiveness. If their goal for "bringing us together" is to reestablish a broad national consensus around the ideas of freedom and self-government that have defined our identity as Americans since the country's founding, no matter how inconsistently applied in our history, we support their efforts. However, if by "bringing us together" people envision a nation that agrees to accept a common set of cultural values and economic approaches as the only path to unity, we respectfully disagree. Not only do we regard the emergence of a new cultural and economic consensus as

---

1 Cox, D., Lienesch, R. and Jones, R.P., *Beyond Economics: Fears of Cultural Displacement Pushed the White Working Class to Trump,* Public Religion Research Institute and The Atlantic Report, May 9, 2017

2 Mounk, Y. and Foa, R. S., *https://www.washingtonpost.com/news/wonk/wp/2016/12/08/ yes-millennials-really-are-surprisingly-approving-of-dictators/,* Washington Post, December 8, 2016

highly unlikely in the coming years, we see the pursuit by groups and communities of varied cultural norms, economic strategies, and locally specific definitions of quality of life as a healthy sign of American freedom and choice. We certainly don't see this diversity in America as an inherently destructive force that requires imposing conformity in life styles to restore a healthy body politic.

The challenge confronting the nation is to find a way to permit our diversity of opinion and action to flourish while restoring faith in the common democratic values and processes that define American self-government and bind us together as a people. Our strategy for achieving this outcome proposes establishing a new civic ethos defining the constellation of rights, responsibilities and arrangements that shape how America is governed. A consensus on what the country's civic ethos should be is central to the proper functioning of our democracy.

AMERICA'S CIVIC ETHOS IN TIME

Whenever the country's future has been in jeopardy and division has threatened the national fabric, as it does now, a new civic ethos has emerged. Over the course of U.S. history there have been three previous times of such intense political crisis or "crucible moments,"[3] each followed by the creation of a new civic ethos, or governing framework.

America's first civic ethos emerged during the transition from thirteen separate colonies to a United States of America, as embodied in the Constitution. It created a national government powerful enough to raise the necessary revenues to "provide for the common defense" and address the infrastructure needs of the fledgling nation. At the same time, many of the states would not agree to grant such centralized power without a promise to provide the protections of individual liberty and the reservation of other powers to the states that became the Bill of Rights. Unfortunately, the country was unable to come to a sustainable consensus on what role the federal government should play in extending those citizenship protections to all who lived within its borders, especially its burgeoning slave population. Only after a terrible civil war and the adoption of the thirteenth, fourteenth, and fifteenth amend-

---

3 The National Task Force on Civic Learning and Democratic Engagement, *A Crucible Moment: College Learning and Democracy's Future,* 2012, Association of American Colleges and Universities.

ments to the Constitution did a second civic ethos emerge that settled the argument over slavery and the assertion of state's rights, in favor of federally-imposed Reconstruction policies, although it took a full century before that federal power was firmly exercised.

Today, America continues to be governed by the next, or third civic ethos--one that emerged from the depths of the Great Depression. The New Deal reflected the public's demand, in the wake of that cataclysmic event, that the scope and purpose of the federal government be extended to managing the nation's economy and assuring that its fruits were widely shared. Presidents from Franklin Roosevelt to Richard Nixon acted on that public expectation to greatly expand the reach and resources of Washington. By 1954, President Dwight Eisenhower correctly observed that, "should any political party attempt to abolish social security, unemployment insurance, and eliminate labor and farm programs, you would not hear of that party again in our political history."[4] In their actions, if not always their rhetoric, more recent Republican presidents—Ronald Reagan and both George Bushes—adhered to Eisenhower's dictum. Although today each party offers its own economic policy prescriptions, they both do so without questioning the underlying public consensus that providing economic prosperity is a critical role of the national government.

America is now in the midst of another time of intense stress on its political and governmental values and institutions. To heal our body politic we need to adopt a new version of America's civic ethos that will once again restore the country's faith in its democratic ideals. We argue that to provide better governance and, in doing so, reinforce the desirability and practicality of our democratic processes, America must replace its increasingly obsolete New Deal civic ethos and its industrial era focus on standardized federal solutions and increasingly elusive national answers to our problems, with a new civic ethos that better reflects the times.

CONSTITUTIONAL LOCALISM SHOULD BE OUR NEXT CIVIC ETHOS

The civic ethos we propose, Constitutional Localism, intentionally shifts the greatest possible number of public decisions to the community level, albeit within a clear Constitutional framework that protects the individual

---

4 Eisenhower, D., *Letter to Edgar Newton Eisenhower*, TeachingAmericanHistory.org

freedoms and rights won over the last 250 years.

Certain responsibilities, such as enforcing and interpreting the Constitution and adhering to that document's assignment of certain responsibilities to the federal government, such as foreign relations, national security, monetary and fiscal policy, and the regulation of inter-state commerce, must remain at their assigned level. States, as well, retain critical responsibilities under their own constitutions and are confronted by issues that must be dealt with on a multi-community basis. However, we see growing evidence that America's diverse communities are successfully displacing states as the new "laboratories of democracy," by finding their own innovative solutions to problems that work best for them.

Given their smaller scale and generally greater cultural, ethnic, and economic homogeneity that makes achieving consensus easier, an expanding number of local communities are fashioning solutions to challenges that elude effective response in Washington and state capitals. Issues related to the environment, economic development, education, the social safety net, crime and health care are being crafted at the local level, with much less controversy and contention than attempts to address the same problems at the federal level. Both economic and social innovations are taking root more readily in localities than at more distant and bureaucratic levels of government.

We believe intentionally supporting a systematic shift of governance from the federal and state levels to communities will offer America two important benefits. In the near term, moving key public decisions to local venues with greater cultural and political homogeneity and smaller scale will result in more successful public responses to citizens' needs that will improve lives.

In the longer term, effective local democratic decision-making will provide the successful governing experiences needed to rebuild the country's belief in democratic decision-making as well as a formula for democratically governing a vast nation with a highly- fragmented set of cultural values and lifestyle preferences.

Not only is our system of Constitutional democracy a proven form of governance for a free people, it is the only acceptable source of unity for the diverse set of citizens who comprise twenty-first century America. This country's uniqueness and the source of much of its success over the past nearly

250 years has come from a national identity that is based on a general acceptance of a set of ideas, rather than upon shared ancestry or religion. Our embrace of an American Idea with its beliefs that "all men are created equal", that "we are endowed" with certain inalienable individual rights, and that democracy as prescribed in the Constitution is the best form of governance for a free people, has provided a nationalism that has bound the American people as powerfully as the call to common blood and religion in the rest of the world. It has also served America well, enabling us to become the only truly universal nation able to successfully integrate peoples from across the globe--a marked advantage for a nation seeking new ideas, energy, and leadership in the global economy. Embracing recent calls to come together, instead, around race, religion, and social beliefs—whether coming from resurgent "nationalist' voices on the right or "identity politics" advocates on both the left and right—will make ever coming together as one people impossible. We either strongly root American identity again in shared democratic values, or we will surely lose our way.

We, the authors, would certainly welcome more national consensus in critical areas of American life--a possibility that seems more likely as we measure the attitudes of the ascending Millennial generation. However, we believe Constitutional Localism offers a way forward, even if our current cultural, social, economic and partisan differences endure.

In a democracy, a civic ethos defines who participates in decisions and the rules of political competition. Given our federal system of government, it also must deal with the distribution of rights between the individual and the government as well as the distribution of power among the layers of government—issues which have animated America's unique quest for civic consensus since its founding. The book that follows is our attempt to make the case for an urgent need to rebalance our current system from the New Deal civic ethos that worked so well for Americans during the Depression and post-War period to a new way of organizing governing rights and responsibilities in our nation.

Before moving on to describe this new civic ethos and elaborate our argument for its adoption, we need to emphasize two elements of Constitutional Localism as we propose it.

First, the "Constitutional" part of Constitutional Localism is central to our belief. We cannot overemphasize our conviction that this increased local preference not be allowed to risk the divisions that would arise from any attempt to undo the historical consensus on individual and civil rights the country has struggled to achieve for 250 years. A bias towards local action cannot be seen as an invitation to individual communities for selective secession from the Constitution. For the shifting of certain public decisions to the local level to work, it must build upon the expansion of rights that so many have fought for in a way that aligns with our Constitution and the Bill of Rights. For this reason we call our proposed new civic ethos Constitutional Localism and believe it is the right way to preserve American democracy in these trying times.

Second, our plea to turn to communities as the new laboratories of democracy and best hope for preserving our democracy is not some temporary expedient to shift key decisions out of Washington during the Trump presidency. The need to find better ways to organize governance in twenty-first century America, both to better solve pressing problems and restore faith in democratic governance, would be just as urgent if Secretary Clinton had won the 2016 presidential election.

MAKING THE CASE

We believe—and history seems to demonstrate—that America periodically needs a new civic ethos to move forward. We think that time has arrived again with the same urgent need to renew American democracy and preserve it for future generations.

Understanding why the New Deal governing paradigm is obsolete and why the Constitutional Localism we propose is an effective replacement must begin with an analysis of what has happened to dramatically alter the conditions confronting American government. In chapter two, we attempt to paint a clear picture of just what changes have occurred in our economy, demography, and culture and why those forces of change have dealt a final blow to the New Deal civic ethos, creating the political gridlock and partisan polarization that constitute our current governing crisis. Chapter three takes a deeper dive to examine the underlying reasons why these forces of change have created our current dilemma, so that we can be sure we are offering a solution that goes to the root of the problem and doesn't just pull up a few weeds to make things look better on the surface.

In chapter four, we more fully define what we mean by Constitutional

Localism and in chapter five we explain why our proposed solution addresses the underlying causes of our current challenge. Chapter six offers examples of local efforts that are already succeeding and suggestions on how to begin to put Constitutional Localism into practice nationally. Finally, chapter seven makes an urgent plea for others to join us in a civic dialogue to accelerate its adoption.

We turn first to the economic events and the government's response to them that triggered the search for a new civic ethos, and then we examine the cultural and demographic revolution that has stirred those economic concerns into a stew of resentment and rebellion that threatens the rules and practices that govern us and our democracy.

CHAPTER TWO:
BREAKDOWN OF THE EXISTING CIVIC ETHOS

The new governing order ushered in by Franklin Roosevelt looked to the federal government for responses to most of America's major challenges and opportunities. It has become obsolete for two reasons. First, we are not the people we were then. World War II movies portrayed Americans of different ethnic groups, although rarely, if ever, African-Americans, working together to achieve victory over the forces of tyranny. But if America ever was a true melting pot, today, the country often appears to be a banquet of separate dishes, each with its own unique and unyielding culture. Second, neither our economy nor our use of technology remotely resembles the mass production, centrally-driven nature of life in the twentieth century. It's not surprising that an earlier governing paradigm has lost its effectiveness given the scope of those changes. What is surprising is the lack of recognition of the impact that the scope and size of these changes has had on our approach to governing America.

In order to judge whether the Constitutional Localism we propose in this book addresses these changes, we need to understand how the ways in which America has changed undermine the assumptions of our current civic ethos and create a new context within which our next civic ethos must fit. We need to have an accurate picture of the variegated composition of America—the nation's vastly changed economy, demographics, culture and politics that has replaced the relative homogeneity of America in the 1930s--in order to ensure our next governing framework will work with, not against, the variety of American life in the twenty-first century.

ECONOMIC SHORTCOMINGS

It is not coincidental that the yearning for a new civic ethos began with the Great Recession in 2008, the worst economic calamity to befall the nation since the 1930s. As captured in the book, *The Big Short*,[5] and the popular movie of the same name, financial malfeasance by banks, credit-rating agencies and other pillars of Wall Street led to the Great Recession, a drastic economic decline that wiped out the jobs and destroyed the assets of millions of Americans. Not only did the newly-loosened regulatory system fail to prevent the disaster, but few, if any, of those who caused the meltdown showed remorse; and none went to jail—even under a Democratic president presumably more inclined to punish "fat cat bankers" than a Republican might have been.[6]

As a result, a sizable portion of the electorate lost its trust in the ability of financial and political elites to manage the country's economic business and look out for the interests of the little guy. A November 2015 Pew Research Center survey found that at least a plurality, if not a majority, of Americans perceived banks (47%), large corporations (56%) and the federal government (67%) to be negative forces in the United States.[7] Those beliefs deeply penetrated our country's politics and undermined the trust in the honesty and competence of those institutions that the New Deal civic ethos depended upon to provide economic stability and prosperity.

Although the monetary policies of the Federal Reserve did save the country from another full-blown depression, and the much-maligned stimulus package passed by the Democratic Congress and signed by President Obama in 2009 did contribute to the unemployment rate dropping by half during his time in office; the recovery produced surprisingly little growth in wages or income for many Americans. According to Bill Galston, "Since 2010, hourly wages corrected for inflation have risen at barely .5% per year." The only way American families could generate more income was by working more hours. Nearly eight years after the end of the Great Recession, median household incomes were a bit lower than in January 2000.[8]

It is important to note, however, that the nation's economy did improve, at least for some people in some parts of the country, starting in 2015,

---

5 Lewis, M., *The Big Short*, W.W. Norton and Company, 2010

6 Schlesinger, J., *Fat Cat Bankers Meet President Obama*, MoneyWatch, December 14, 2009

7 *Beyond Distrust: How Americans View Their Government*, Pew Research Center, November 23, 2015

8 Galston, B., *An Econ Mystery: Why Did Wages Flatline?* Wall Street Journal, May 9, 2017

a full year before the earthshaking election of 2016. In 2015, according to the Bureau of the Census, median household incomes, even after considering inflation, rose 5.2%; they increased another 3.2% during the presidential election year of 2016. In those same two years, wages began rising at a faster pace, and the poverty rate began its continuing fall. The country also experienced a lessening of income inequality with the share of national income going to workers rising and the share going to investors falling.

Data from the latest Survey of Consumer Finances by the Federal Reserve Board, shows a similar trend based on the net worth, or total value of assets owned, of all households since 2013. Much of the growth came from demographics that are normally at the lower end of the socioeconomic scale. African American families experienced an almost 30% increase in their net worth, Hispanic families enjoyed an eye-popping 46% increase; and families headed by those with only a high school diploma saw their net worth rise by an average of 24%. Still, economic inequality remained a source of envy and concern. The net worth of families headed by those with college degrees rose only 2%. However, the average net worth of such households was still four times that of households headed by those without a college degree.[9]

One reason why the economy doesn't appear to have improved for many working-class Americans is that most of the gains in both income and net worth were attributable to the fact that many Americans worked more hours in a tightening labor market, not because of a sudden surge in wages or economic growth. But, there is another aspect of our recent economic recovery from the Great Recession that was not part of the country's economic experience after the Great Depression and World War II.

The return to economic prosperity in some regions and in some industries, has not been felt in others, creating wildly different views on the future of America's economy and what to do about it. The localized and uneven nature of America's economic recovery is partially, if not predominantly, caused by the "inherent tendency," as economist Enrico Moretti puts it, toward geographic agglomeration of the information technology sector, the most powerful engine of innovation in our new economy. This means that the current national economy heavily favors those cities with the "right" industries and deep pools of well-educated workers able to compete for jobs with high

---

9 Long, H. and Jan, T. *https://www.washingtonpost.com/news/wonk/wp/2017/09/27/since-2013-minorities-and-americans-without-college-degrees-showed-greatest-gains-in-wealth-federal-reserve-report-shows/* Washington Post, September 27, 2017.

wages, while those cities with the "wrong industries and a limited human capital base," are stuck with dead-end jobs and low average wages. The divide is what Moretti calls the "Great Divergence," and it is exacerbating not just the nation's economic fissures but its political divisions as well.[10]

Results from the last election in communities across the Midwest Rust Belt illustrate how the country's "lumpy" economic performance has contributed to its political divide. As John Austin pointed out in a study for the Brookings Institution, "The small- and medium-sized factory towns that dot the highways and byways of Michigan, Indiana, Ohio and Wisconsin have lost their anchor employers and are struggling to fill the void. Many of these communities, including once solidly Democratic-voting, union-heavy, blue collar strongholds, flipped to Trump in 2016."[11]

For example, in Michigan's rural counties and in those containing smaller industrial cities, such as Battle Creek, Bay City, Jackson and Saginaw, that have not kept up with the changing economy, Trump won by large margins. The Democratic candidate, Hillary Clinton, carried the Detroit metropolitan area but not much else. She did win the two outstate counties with major research universities in them, but the only other outstate county she carried was one with a city, Kalamazoo, that had focused its economic revival on an innovative approach to expanding educational opportunity. The end result was an almost even split in that state's vote, with Trump's approximately ten thousand vote margin adding to his string of upset victories in other similarly situated Midwest battleground states.

America's economy has also shifted in the type of jobs and industries that pay good wages. The number of Americans working in manufacturing peaked in 1979; mining employment, including oil, gas and coal extraction, peaked in 1982. In 1965 these two blue-collar occupations, along with construction, provided about one out of three non-agricultural jobs in the U.S. Today, they provide fewer than one in seven. This dramatic change in the occupational makeup of the American work force has had an especially profound impact on the employment prospects of people without a college education or other post-secondary skill training.[12]

10 Moretti, E., The New Geography of Jobs, Houghton Mifflin Harcourt, 2012

11 Austin, J., A Tale of Two Rust Belts: Diverging Economic Paths Shaping Community Politics, Brookings Institution, June 30, 2017

12 Brownstein, R., Rusty Lever Won't Lift U.S. Economy, Los Angeles Times, June 9, 2017

Rob Shapiro, CEO of Sonecon, examined household employment data from the Bureau of Labor Statistics and found that Americans with college degrees accounted for all the net new jobs created over the last decade. In stark contrast, the number of Americans with high school diplomas or less who were employed has fallen by 2,995,000 since the Great Recession. Even as late as December 2017, the data showed the number of college graduates with jobs jumped that month by 305,000, but the numbers of employed Americans with no high school diploma fell by 132,000, the number of high school graduates with jobs dropped by 38,000, and the number of employees with some college but no degree declined by 45,000.[13]

There are also generational and gender differences in how well America's economy is working. Beginning in 1967, lifetime earnings of younger men began to decline compared to those of older cohorts. This is the best indicator we have of the "end of the American Dream" when children would no longer do better financially than their parents. Although this was not immediately the case for women, because of the differences in workforce participation between men and women during these same decades, the same trend has become evident recently for female lifetime incomes. Studies show the problem is caused by the lower starting salaries and wages of twenty-five -year olds as they enter the workforce. Starting much farther behind in the race for lifetime income, they never catch up. And because of the nature of our information age economy, the need for increased levels of education to get good jobs is the "single most important reason this problem exists," according to Ron Haskins, senior fellow at the Brookings Institute. "You have to have better skills and more knowledge to make $60,000 to $80,000 a year now than in the past."[14]

In summary, much of the economic pain and disappointment many Americans feel, even as others bask in the prosperity of a rising stock market and high-tech economy, is real and justified. Populism, whether it comes from the left or right, captures people's anger at these economic disparities but does little to provide solutions to the underlying problems. There is no way to reverse the steady loss of high-wage, low-skill jobs in an increasingly

---

13 Shapiro, R., *The New Economics of Jobs Is Bad News for Working Class Americans —and Maybe for Trump, https://www.brookings.edu/blog/fixgov/2018/01/16/the-new-economics-of-jobs-is-bad-news-for-working-class-americans-and-maybe-for-trump/,* GOP, Jan 18, 2016

14 Cohen, P., New York Times, *https://www.nytimes.com/2017/09/16/business/economy/ bump-in-us-incomes-doesnt-erase-50-years-of-pain.html,* September 16, 2017

automated, global economy built on the value of information and knowledge, as much as some may wish it. Nor can economic policies, rooted in the New Deal's belief that the central government can maintain a uniformly vigorous and equitable economy, fully address these concerns through government intervention in an increasingly "lumpy" economy. Instead, we need a new synthesis of our economic and political systems to enable economic growth in all of the nation's communities, which, in today's America, can only come through a more bottom-up approach.

DEMOGRAPHICS, CULTURE AND THE CHANGING FACE OF AMERICA

The lack of faith in democracy so many Americans express today is not solely a reaction to bad economic times. Indeed, if that were the case, a revival of the country's faith in its government and its leaders should have occurred as the economy gathered significant momentum during the last few years. That it did not is the result of other equally powerful forces at play—demographic and cultural changes, which have been creating cracks in the New Deal consensus for decades and continue to do so today.

Since the 1930's, when the New Deal was born, the U.S. population has evolved from one that was almost entirely white, Christian and of European descent, to one that represents all of the world's races and most of its nationalities and religions (or, recently, lack of religion). In large part, the civic crisis that confronts the nation today is a reaction to this increased diversity.

In 1930, 90% of Americans were white. African Americans, 80% of whom lived in the South, comprised virtually all of those who weren't. Barely 1% were "Mexican" (the only census designation for Hispanics then); less than half as many were "Asian-American" (a designation that would not be used by the Census Bureau until 1980).[15] By 2016, the white share of the U.S. population had fallen to 61% while that of African-Americans had increased slightly to 13%. Hispanics at 18% had become the country's largest "minority"; Asian-Americans, who had barely registered eight decades earlier, comprised 6% of the nation.[16]

---

15 *Historical Census Statistics on Population Totals by Race 1790 to 1990 for the United States Regions, Divisions, and States,* U.S. Census Bureau, www.census.gov

16 *Quick Facts, Population Estimates,* U.S. Census Bureau, July 1, 2016

In 1930, about one-third of those living in the United States were immigrants or their children.[17] But unlike today back then, almost 90% of first and second-generation Americans were of European descent. Now, 50% of first and second-generation Americans are of Latin American heritage, while 27% are Asian and 7% are African or Middle Eastern. Today, European immigrants and their children comprise only 12%.[18]

The trend toward a more diverse and different United States seems certain to continue. Millennials, America's largest adult cohort born between 1982 and 2003, are 40% non-white. By 2020, a majority of American children are expected to be non-white; the nation as a whole is projected to reach that milestone around 2044.[19] Members of the generation born after Millennials, whom we call Plurals to reflect the fact that theirs is a generation without a racial or ethnic majority, will grow up having experienced only a majority-minority America. Even as some in America celebrate this increasing diversity, others fear its damage to traditional American values and fume over its inevitability.

It is important to remember that one particular aspect of America's racial and ethnic composition—the position of African Americans in the country's society—is of ongoing concern and predates the creation of the United States. Although the percentage of blacks in the country's population has changed only slightly since the 1930s, the issues of discrimination and inequality remain. For the most part, the New Deal ignored the challenge of equal rights for all Americans in order to gain political support for its new economic program. In the decades that followed World War II, a reenergized civil rights movement emerged that sought to guarantee the nation's racial and ethnic minorities full citizenship rights in every part of the United States. Those efforts produced legislation and court decisions that expanded educational opportunities, increased electoral participation and improved economic opportunities for African-Americans.[20] The election of a black president, something that was inconceivable as recently as the 1950s, further indicates

---

17 *Nativity and Percentage of the Population, 1790 to 1930, 1960, and 1970,* U.S. Census Bureau, March 9, 1999

18 *Second-Generation Americans: A Portrait of the Adult Children of Immigrants,* Pew Research Center, February 7, 2013

19 *New Census Bureau Report Analyzes U.S. Population Projections,* United States Census Bureau Press Release, March 3, 2015

20 *Black Demographics, The African-American Middle Class, http://blackdemographics. com/households/middle-class/* 2012

the depth of the cultural change in America since the creation of the New Deal civic ethos.[21] But, as today's battles over police tactics demonstrate, the issue of the position of African-Americans in U.S. society is far from resolved, and many white and black Americans, as well as Hispanics, continue to experience the country differently.

Along with its racial and ethnic demographics, America's religious composition has diversified and, to an extent, broken down over the past eight decades. Although there is no way of knowing precisely the denominational breakdown of the U.S. population in 1930, Gallup has polled that matter since 1948. In its first survey, 91% of Americans were Christian, of whom 69% were Protestant (a percentage that included non-denominational Christians and Mormons), and 22% were Catholic. An additional 4% were Jewish. Less than 1% affiliated with some other faith, and only 2% were willing to say that they had no religious attachment. In Gallup's 2016 survey, the number of Christians had fallen to 71%, with Protestants accounting for the entire decline. Bolstered by Latin American immigration, the percentage of Catholics remained at 22%, while the percentage of Jews dropped by half, to 2%. By contrast, affiliation with other faiths increased to 5%, with Hindus and Muslims being the largest contributors. But the greatest change was the nine-fold increase, to 18%, in those claiming no religious affiliation.[22] The number of "nones" (to use the Pew Research term for those with no denominational connection) is almost certain to rise in the future; more than a third of Millennials say they have no religious affiliation.[23] Whether America ever was, or ever should have been, bound together as a nation by a common religious faith, it is clear no such common ground exists today.

Accompanying these changes in our nation's demographics has been a dramatic exodus from rural communities to urban environments. Americans have been moving from the countryside to urbanized areas since the founding of the nation, but as late as 1930, almost half the population (46%) still lived in a rural area (defined as a place with less than 2500 people), and less than half (45%) in a "metropolitan area" (defined as a locality containing an urban core with a population of at least fifty thousand). More than two-thirds of those metropolitan residents lived in a central city, rather than a sub-

---

21 Gallup News, *The Presidency, http://new.gallup.com/poll/4729/presidency.aspx*

22 Gallup Historical Trends, In Depth: Topics A to Z- Religion

23 *America's Changing Religious Landscape,* Pew Research Center, May 12, 2015

urb.[24] In 2015, 86% of the country lived in a metro area, and the proportions residing in central cities and suburbs had been reversed. Now, a majority of Americans (53%) are suburbanites.[25] This dramatic shift from the country side and small towns to the cities and suburbs has been accompanied by a growing cultural separation between the rest of the country and rural America, reflected by such unlikely developments as the emergence of an online dating service restricted to those who live on a farm or in a small town.

In terms of sheer numbers, the most notable transformation has been in the role women play in our society. In 1930, only one-quarter of American women—the large majority of whom were unmarried—worked outside of the home, and women comprised just 22% of the workforce.[26] Most employed women held domestic service, clerical or sales positions. The minority with professional jobs were primarily public-school teachers or nurses. By 2014, a majority of women (57%) worked for pay and comprised nearly half (47%) of the labor force; 70% of women who have children younger than 18 years old are now working outside of the home.[27] While most women continue to work in traditionally "female" occupations, fully half of U.S. professional and managerial employees now are women, including more than one- third in such longtime male bastions as dentistry, law, and medicine.[28] By 2013, women comprised 13% of those in law enforcement[29] and, two years later, 15% of active-duty military personnel.[30] Now, the #metoo movement is seeking to ensure equal treatment of women in every part of the workforce--the next step in this unprecedented cultural transformation. But its very existence demonstrates that when it comes to attitudes toward gender, America is not yet one country.

Perhaps the most dramatic recent societal change has been the advancement of gay rights. In the 1930s, and for decades thereafter, homo-

---

24 Hobbs, F. and Stoops, N., *Demographic Trends in the 20th Century: Census 2000 Special Reports,* U.S. Census Bureau, November 2002

25 Kolko, J. *How Suburban are Big American Cities?* FiveThirtyEight, May 21, 2015

26 *Women in the Labor Force,* U.S. Department of Labor, Women's Bureau

27 Ibid

28 *Household Data Annual Averages: Employed Persons by Detailed Occupation, Sex, Race, and Hispanic or Latino Identity,* Bureau of Labor Statistics

29 *Women in Law Enforcement,* Community Policy Dispatch Volume 6, Issue 7, July, 2013

30 Johnson, D. and Stamp, B., *See Women's Progress in the U.S. Military,* Time Labs, September 8, 2015

sexuality was illegal nationwide. But in 2003, a Supreme Court decision ruled state anti-sodomy laws unconstitutional, and 8 years later, prodded by Vice President Biden, the Obama administration decided to permit gays to serve openly in the U.S. armed forces. Only four years later, the Supreme Court legalized same-sex marriage across the nation. The speed and magnitude of these changes in our country's attitudes and laws left Millenials and many other groups, both inside and outside the gay community, overjoyed; others, particularly Evangelical Protestants, were dismayed at this shift in our cultural norms.

These major transformations in the composition of America's population and its culture has made the country a very different nation in this century than it was in the last. In many important ways, the changes have created two distinct cultures that are barely able to talk to each other much less find common ground.

Cultural change inevitably creates political disruption, which in turn requires new political solutions to create an effective governing structure. As the late Senator Daniel Patrick Moynihan stated, "The central conservative truth is that it is culture, not politics, that determines the success of a society. The central liberal truth is that politics can change a culture and save it from itself."[31] Unfortunately, a civic ethos built upon New Deal assumptions of a homogeneous and stable population does not appear to be up to the task of creating a politics capable of overcoming these divisions.

INTENSIFYING PARTISANSHIP, POLARIZATION, GRIDLOCK AND DISSATISFACTION WITH THE FEDERAL GOVERNMENT

A Pew survey conducted two months before the 2016 general election described the recent evolution of party identification in the United States as "two coalitions, moving further apart."[32] To a disproportionate and growing degree, the Republican "coalition"—centered on white voters, especially males; those without college degrees; Evangelical Protestants; and older voters —mirrors America's population as it was when the last civic ethos was created. By contrast, the Democratic "coalition"—based largely on women,

---

31 Moynihan, D.P. and Weisman, S. (ed.), *Daniel P. Moynihan: A Portrait in Letters of an American Visionary,* Hachette Book Group, 2010

32 *The Parties on the Eve of the 2016 Election: Two Coalitions, Moving Further Apart,* Pew Research Center, September 2016

racial, ethnic, and religious minorities, Millennials, college graduates, and those unaffiliated with a specific religious faith—reflects many of the changes the country has experienced since the New Deal. The political slogans of the two presidential candidates in 2016 reflected the two coalitions' increasingly-distinctive views on what should be done about these changes going forward. The Democratic candidate talked about being "stronger together" and the Republican about "Making America Great Again." If these partisan divisions, and the increased diversity they reflect, were distributed evenly across the United States, their political impact might be less, or at least different than, it has been. But, as the Pew study indicates, they are not.

The divisions are particularly pronounced at the local level. Residents of urban areas, which are relatively diverse in their racial, ethnic, and religious composition and are younger in age, now identify as Democrats over Republicans by a nearly 2:1 ratio (60% to 33%). Those living in rural areas, which are disproportionately white, Christian and older, identify as Republicans over Democrats by almost as great a margin (55% to 37%). The suburbs, which were once seen as an upscale and white Republican bastion, are now more varied in their make-up. As a result, they have become the real battleground of American electoral politics, almost evenly divided between Republican (48%) and Democratic (44%) partisans.[33]

The political impact of these demographic shifts has become magnified in Congress, particularly in the U.S. House of Representatives, which is designed to reflect local, not national or even state, concerns. Like two heavyweight boxers returning to their separate corners after every round of fighting, each party has concentrated more and more of its resources after each election to representing and reflecting the interests of its base. In the 115th Congress that first met in January 2017, 95% of Congressional Republicans were white, 96% were Christian (including 72% Protestant), and 91% were male. Reflecting their party's make up, Congressional Democrats were more diverse. Four in ten were members of a minority racial or ethnic group and women comprised a like percentage. One in five identified with a non-Christian religious tradition.[34] The result has been a growing polarization within Congress and an inability of the institution to enact legislation to deal with the issues of most concern to Americans.

---

33 Ibid

34 *Demographics of Members of Congress,* Brookings Institution, 2017

The ideological split between the two parties has widened each decade since the post-World War II period. From the late 1940s through the 1950s, the average ideological position of both parties in each chamber clustered around the centrist midpoint. From the 1960s through the 1980s, the voting scores of both parties in each house increased to somewhat more ideologically-defined positions. Since then, the ideological voting of both parties, especially Republicans, has risen dramatically. One calculation, by political scientists Keith Poole and Howard Rosenthal, shows that during the final three Congresses of the Obama presidency, Democrats had grown even more liberal and Republicans more conservative in their voting, creating the widest ideological gap ever between the congressional parties.[35]

This level of polarization, accompanied by the heightened partisanship reflective of the diverging nature of the country's two major party coalitions, has produced a level of gridlock in the country's governing institutions not seen since the days leading up to the Civil War. Data assembled by the Brookings Institution indicates that in the two post-World War II Congresses, when consensus on the New Deal civic ethos was greatest, about one-quarter (23%) of the bills introduced in the House of Representatives passed that body. In the more collegial Senate, a majority (53%) did. Even as recently as the 1990s about one-quarter of the Senate and 14% of House bills cleared their respective chambers, while in the second decade of the twenty-first century, just 10% of House bills and 15% of Senate bills did.[36] This level of inaction further undermines the nation's former embrace of the New Deal civic ethos, which relies upon effective and efficient federal decision-making to work.

The toll on perceptions of Congress, the branch of the federal government at the heart of gridlock, has been particularly profound. Since 1973, Gallup has been asking the public to indicate the level of its confidence in Congress. In its initial survey, a strong plurality (42%) said it had a "great deal" or "quite a lot" of confidence, while only 14% had "very little" or "none." That was the high-water mark in the electorate's confidence in the federal legislative branch. While it has fluctuated a bit over time, the trend for the past four decades has been downward. Since 2006, at least twice as many Americans have had negative, rather than positive, attitudes toward Con-

35 *Political Polarization in Congress and Changing Voting Alignments,* Brookings Institution, 2017

36 *Legislative Productivity in Congress and Workload,* Brookings Institution, 2017

gress on this measure. In Gallup's three most recent studies (2014-2016) majorities have had "very little" or "no" confidence in Congress, while fewer than one-in-ten have had "a great deal" or "quite a lot."[37]

Public attitudes toward U.S. presidents almost invariably have been more positive than those toward Congress. Still, presidential job approval ratings, the standard measure of voter satisfaction with the chief executive, have also trended downward since the 1950s and 1960s.

A Pew analysis indicates that both Eisenhower and Kennedy averaged above 80% approval from voters who identified with the president's party, but also 49% approval from those who identified with the opposition party. By contrast, presidents from Reagan to Obama, while still averaging 81% approval from their own partisans, received positive marks from only 28% on average of identifiers with the opposing party.[38] A similar pattern of partisan attitudes toward the president has been evident in President Trump's approval ratings since the beginning of his presidency. His 39% overall approval in Pew's first measurement was based on an 84% approval among Republicans, but only 8% among Democrats, something that remained relatively stable throughout his first year in the White House.[39]

The declines in positive attitudes toward both the Congress and the presidency have led to a lessening of "political efficacy," the belief by citizens that they can influence what government does. For sixty years, the American National Election Studies (ANES) has measured the U.S. electorate's perception of its ability to impact government decisions by asking voters if they agreed or disagreed that "people like me don't have any say in what the government does." From 1952 through 1964, roughly seven-in-ten Americans disagreed. Declining majorities held that belief through the 1990s, but in the current century at least a plurality have believed that ordinary citizens have little say in the actions of government. Nearly half (48%) did so in 2012, the last time the ANES survey results on the question were reported.[40] This disconnect between the federal government and those it governs undermines

---

37 Gallup Historical Trends, In Depth: Topics A to Z- Congress and the Public

38 *Political Polarization in the American Public, Section 2: Growing Partisan Antipathy,* Pew Research Center, June 12, 2014

39 *In First Month, Views of Trump are Already Strongly Felt, Deeply Polarized,* Pew Research Center, February 16, 2017

40 *People Don't Have a Say in What Government Does, 1952-2012,* The ANES Guide to Public Opinion and Electoral Behavior

support for a New Deal civic ethos dependent on major governmental action at the national level to solve problems.

Ominously, the failure of our current civic ethos, and the resulting fall in confidence in government and the ability of the average citizen to influence it, has caused most Americans to lose faith in the country's future. Since 1988, Pew Research has been asking Americans to state their level of satisfaction with the way things are going. Except for a brief interregnum as the country rallied after the 9/11 attacks, a growing majority has expressed its dissatisfaction with the state of the nation; over the past decade at least two-thirds of the country has felt that way.[41] In 2015, Pew found that fewer than half (45%) of the U. S. had "a lot" of confidence in the future of the United States; 15% had little or none.[42]

A country without confidence in its future is especially susceptible to attacks on its fundamental values and principles. This is particularly dangerous for one held together solely by its common values and belief in democracy. The failure of the federal government to address the country's challenges has caused too many American citizens to question their faith in democratic decision-making and rules of behavior and, indeed, in the American idea itself.

Enumerating the political divisions that have been created by the changes in our economy, demographics, and culture is the first step in understanding the divisions that have rendered our current civic ethos obsolete. However, before the right remedy is offered for the current clear and present danger to democracy that such divisions pose, it is important to first examine the underlying forces that are causing these changes. Only then can we measure the degree to which the solution we propose, or any alternative, addresses the totality of the challenge.

---

41 *Public Trust in Government Remains at Historic Lows as Partisan Attitudes Shift,* Pew Research Center, May 3, 2017

42 *Beyond Distrust: How Americans View Their Government, 8. Perceptions of the Public's Voice in Government and Politics,* Pew Research Center, November 23, 2015

CHAPTER THREE:
CAUSES OF THE BREAKDOWN

The cultural, demographic, social, and economic changes the United States has experienced in the past eighty years are real and not simply a figment of pundits' imaginations. Given the magnitude of the changes that have occurred in a relatively short time span, it is to be expected that many Americans are anxious about the transformation of our demographics and culture, while others applaud it. New communications technologies help to further fragment us into competing tribes, based on our values and partisan passions. It is hardly surprising that some want the political system and government to endorse and further the changes, while others want those institutions to slow or even reverse them. Because these changes appear to threaten deeply-held values on one side of the dispute or the other, whatever action government might take becomes a source for distrust of government and our democratic decision-making process as a whole.

However, before we can postulate a new civic ethos that will respond to these dramatic shifts in a way that renews the country's faith in democracy, we need to understand the underlying causes of the changes we have experienced. It is one thing to conclude that the old order no longer works but quite another to determine what will work in our new national circumstances. To accomplish that task, we first have to identify the forces propelling the changes that must be accommodated and leveraged in order to ensure that Constitutional Localism is the best path for America to take going forward.

DIVERGING AMERICAN VALUES

The increasing variety of America's demographic composition makes it difficult to forge agreement on the most fundamental aspect of a nation's culture—its values. Although it is almost impossible to change an individual's values once they have been embraced as an adult, that does not preclude the country from reaching an agreement on its public values. That task has become much more challenging than in the past, because the range of personal values held by Americans has widened significantly over the past three decades.

In the initial Pew Research Values Surveys, beginning in 1987, partisan divisions were relatively muted on cultural and social issues.[43] Republicans were not strikingly more conservative, nor were Democrats sharply more liberal on attitudes toward governmental efforts to ensure equal rights for African Americans and other minorities, women's and gay rights, support for traditional values, and immigration and its impact on America, as well as the extent to which Americans held traditional religious beliefs. All of which seems inconceivable in light of today's culture wars.

Twenty-five years later partisan polarization on cultural issues, especially those relating to race and ethnicity, had widened significantly. By 2012, the two parties' identifiers were separated to a greater extent on these matters, just as they had been on economic issues a quarter of a century earlier.[44] Between 1994 and 2017, Pew Research showed that the gap between how Republicans and Democrats responded to the statement, "Blacks who can't get ahead in this country are mostly responsible for their own condition" had more than doubled (from 13 to 47 percentage points). Similarly, over the same period, the partisan division among those perceiving that "Immigrants today are a burden on our country because they take our jobs, housing, and health care" had widened from 2 to 32 points; and the difference between Republican and Democratic identifiers agreeing that "homosexuality should be discouraged by society" grew from 16 to 24 points.[45]

This polarization on cultural issues was still evident in surveys taken during the 2016 election. In a survey taken the week before the election, 79% of Trump voters, as compared to 20% of Clinton voters, perceived "illegal immigration" to be a problem. By contrast, Clinton voters were far more likely than Trump voters to believe that "sexism" and "racism" were serious national concerns.[46]

The growing inclination of Americans to live in places where most of

---

43 *http://www.people-press.org/files/2012/06/Appendix.pdf*

44 Ibid

45 *The Partisan Gap on Political Values Grows Even Wider,* Pew Research Center, October 5, 2017

46 A *Divided and Pessimistic Electorate,* Pew Research Center, November 10, 2016

their neighbors are likely to share their values, if not their ethnicity and religious beliefs, also makes finding a national consensus on values difficult. In 2014, Pew indicated that 77% of those considered "consistently liberal" and 57% of those labeled "mostly liberal" preferred to live in communities where "the houses are smaller and closer to each other, but schools, stores, and restaurants are within walking distance." By contrast, three-fourths of respondents designated as "consistent conservatives" and two-thirds of those rated "mostly conservative" wanted to live in places where "the houses are larger and farther apart, but schools, stores, and restaurants are several miles away." When given the hypothetical option of "living anywhere in the United States," 67% of "consistent liberals" and 55% of those "mostly liberal" said they would prefer to live in either a city or a suburb, while 76% of "consistent conservatives" and 66% of "mostly conservative" répondants would choose to reside in a small town or rural area. A majority of liberals also said that it is important for them to live in a place containing "a mix of people from different racial and ethnic backgrounds," while most conservatives place importance on living where "many share [their] religious faith."[47]

As understandable and traditional as the preference for living among people who share similar attitudes and beliefs may be, its impact on political polarization creates just one more obstacle to building national consensus. In the 2016 presidential election, the margin between the parties was greater than 20 percentage points in almost two-thirds of U.S. counties. This was a complete reversal of the 1992 results, when the partisan division was less than 20 percentage points in two-thirds of the counties.[48] The website 538, created by mathematics guru, Nate Silver, uses statistical analysis to help readers better understand politics and elections. It summarized its findings by asserting that "purple counties" (those that were closely divided in their partisanship) have "all but disappeared."

This localized electoral polarity, underpinned by demographic concentrations of distinctive cultures, helps explain our current difficulty in forging the broad consensus around critical issues facing the country at the federal level. It also points out the need for a new civic ethos that is not dependent on a broad, national consensus for it to work.

---

47 *Political Polarization in the American Public, Section 3. Political Polarization and Personal Life,* Pew Research Center, June 12, 2014

48 Wasserman, D., *Purple America Has All but Disappeared,* FiveThirtyEight, March 8, 2017

A REVOLUTION IN COMMUNICATION TECHNOLOGIES

Relationships and interactions between individuals in this increasingly ethnically and culturally diverse nation have been altered, and our differences amplified, by the emergence of qualitatively different communications technologies. Social media has emerged as a major force, seemingly pulling the country apart in different directions by providing a platform for the most vitriolic and divisive rhetoric to infect the body politic.

Although people used to think of it as a toy to entertain Millennials, President Trump's use of Twitter has demonstrated the power this new communication-technology architecture has to influence voters and drive our political debate. The impact of Trump's tweets is an excellent example of how social media have transformed the relatively-languid pace of news reporting based on the day's events into a continuous torrent of news of widely-varying value, targeted at very different and distinct audiences.

Each political era in America has witnessed the impact of a new communication technology that has reinforced the political behavior of its time. In the fiery, partisan world of the nineteenth century, people chose which daily newspaper to read based on the political view of its editorial page. By 1870, 90% of the daily newspapers in America's fifty largest cities used a partisan filter in presenting their news and information. But their reach, for the most part, was local, and their ability to shape national political debates was limited as a result.[49]

Early in the twentieth century, however, newspapers were faced with competition from a brand-new communication technology that was able to broadcast a signal across long distances, enabling first radio, then television, to reach much larger audiences and to garner a greater and greater share of advertising budgets from their national corporate sponsors. Unlike local newspapers that relied on a combination of subscriptions and advertising for their revenue, national broadcast networks depend strictly on advertising revenue to sustain themselves.

Given its need for the largest audience possible, the business model of broadcast networks required a more neutral, objective posture to make sure no member of the audience was offended by what they heard and no sponsor was criticized for the programming it put "on the air" under its name.

---

49 Winograd, M. and Hais, M.D., *Millennial Makeover,* Rutgers University Press, 2008

The networks brand image as the source for objective, expert news and information became so powerful in the 1960s that President Johnson was reported to have said the Vietnam War was lost when Walter Cronkite came out against it on his nightly CBS News broadcast.[50]

The effect of national media outlets seeking broad audiences and a safe place for advertisers was the emergence of network brands that placed reliable, objective expertise above partisan politics. The result was, to a degree never experienced before, a uniform national popular culture that contributed to a lessening of partisan animosity and an increase in patriotic unity for several decades after the Great Depression and World War II.[51] It was the perfect communication technology to support the development of the progressive model of centralized and objective government perfected by President Roosevelt in the New Deal.

Today, the three pillars of "traditional media"— newspapers, radio, and television—that dominated our country's culture in the twentieth century are losing their audience to a brand-new communication architecture: social media. These networks move the source of expertise from the earlier, centralized sources of power to the wisdom of crowds, gathered into groups on the Internet, formed at the initiation of like-minded users without guidance from any authority.

Unlike broadcast networks, the Internet, from its inception, was an open system designed for sharing information. Social media takes advantage of this property to allow anyone, anywhere, to say anything, at any time, to anyone who will pay attention. Once the number of Internet users reached critical mass, and Internet connection speeds became fast enough to share visual, as well as text media, social media's popularity took off. Only 7% of the country used social networking sites in 2005; just a decade later, it had become a part of the lives of two-thirds of the American public.[52]

A Pew survey taken in 2016 suggested that this is only the beginning of the transformation. Overall, Americans are still more likely to "often" get their news from television than online (57% to 40%). But demographics speak to the fragility of those TV numbers. Although solid majorities of those aged

50 University of Oregon, Media by the Decades Project—The 1960's, *Walter Cronkite: The Most Trusted Man in America. https://blogs.uoregon.edu/frengsj387/vietnam-war/*

51 Turchin, P. *Ages of Discord,* Beresta Books, 2016

52 *Social Media Usage 2005-2015,* Pew Research Center, October 8, 2015

50-64 (72%) and 65+ (85%) often view news on TV, far smaller shares of younger adults do so (45% of those 30-49 and 27% of those 18-29). A 2016 Pew survey suggested that this is only the beginning of the transformation. The two younger groups of adults are much more likely than older adults to turn to online platforms for news instead—50% of 18-29-year-olds and 49% of those 30-49. Moreover, those young adults, particularly the 18-29-year-olds, were as likely to utilize social media networking sites as sources for their news, as they were websites specifically designed for that purpose.[53]

Social media represent a brand-new and dramatically-different communication architecture, allowing "many to many" communications at practically no cost. Whereas broadcast media use a "one to many" design, social media allow everyone to be both producer and consumer of news and information, with time, rather than money, being the major constraint to their usage. In such a world, authority depends on the number of people who follow a website or social network page, not upon one's credentials or expertise. This qualitative and quantitative difference has immense implications for America's civic culture and for its political debate.

At its core, the Internet is an inherently dis-intermediating technology. In other words, it allows for a more direct interaction between consumers and producers, or candidates and voters, without the filter of editorial preferences or expertise. When that capability is combined with the ability of social networks to easily link people into communities with mutual interests, the possibility for the creation of echo chambers, in which people only hear what other people who look, or act, or think like them have to say, increases dramatically. Instead of counting on intrepid journalists or nightly news anchors to bring to the audience's attention news of places or people who think and act differently, social networks bring the comfort of consensus to their users. In such an environment, what is "true" becomes what the group believes to be true, and "fake news" becomes anything that doesn't fit the group's predetermined point of view.

Lately, the ability of companies to scour an individual's social media pages on Facebook and other such platforms has created the opportunity to market products to a much more targeted audience— one that is more likely to be interested in the product—rather than to employ the scattershot nature

---

53 *The Modern News Consumer: News Attitudes and Practices in the Digital Era*, Pew Research Center, July 2016

of broadcast-media advertising. In politics, this approach, first used by President Obama's campaign in 2008 and enhanced with even more sophisticated algorithms by Cambridge Analytica in President Trump's campaign, has created the possibility that voters might "only hear what they want to hear" for an entire campaign, no matter what the opposition might say or do.[54]

A free and independent press has been recognized as a key element of a functioning democracy since the adoption of the First Amendment to the Constitution. Social media's circumvention of any intermediating editorial role leaves its users with little ability to determine where expertise lies and whom to believe. This change in how Americans absorb news and information and share it with others has enormous implications for how we shape a new civic ethos and helps explain why the old one isn't working.

Even if it were possible to ban Facebook, Twitter, Instagram, Snap Chat and other popular social networks that may undermine the ability to find objective sources of alternative points of view in our public life, such an effort would be extremely unwise. The potential of social media to enable infinite, lateral communication also brings with it the possibility for a much greater degree of cooperation within every community in the country and across the globe. When further enhanced with the newest in virtual-reality technologies, social media also has the potential to create the ultimate empathetic experience--greatly increasing our ability to literally, or at least virtually, "walk in the other person's shoes."[55] Rather than vilify the two of every three Americans who use social media multiple times every day, civic leaders need to find new ways to use its power to improve how our democracy functions and to create new ways to help citizens distinguish fact from fiction.

Social media must become enablers of our efforts to find common purpose, not obstacles. The profound ability of the new communication media to shape the environment in which we seek effective solutions to public problems must be considered by the proponents of any civic ethos purporting to restore the efficacy of civic engagement. These new technologies are more than passing fads; they are democratic game changers, whose impact must be harnessed to help make democracy work better.

---

54 Cadwalladr, C., *Robert Mercer: The Big Data Billionaire Waging War on Mainstream Media*, Guardian, February 26, 2017

55 Engroff, J. *The Ultimate Empathy Machine: VR and Social*, MediaPost, March 10, 2017

THE FAILURE OF NEW DEAL ECONOMICS

A nation's economic growth is the arithmetic product of the changes in its population and productivity (annual output increase per hour worked in the non-farm sector).[56] Unlike many other industrialized nations, the United States enjoyed a burst of population growth in the final two decades of the last century, as Boomers and members of Generation X had babies in sufficient numbers to make the Millennial generation the largest in the nation's history. Birth rates declined, however, in the face of economic uncertainty after the Great Recession. Meanwhile, Millennials delayed their own parenting experiences, burdened by unprecedented levels of student debt and by the desire of more-and-more educated women to pursue careers rather than "settle down and have children."

As Boomers retire in record numbers over the next two decades, the number of U.S.-born workers with U.S.-born parents will fall by 8.2 million people, leading to a reduction in the growth rate of the country's working-age population to levels not seen in decades. The only way to replace these workers is through immigration by working-age adults--a prospect that is at the center of Trump voters' discontent. However, over the next two decades, without an influx of immigrant workers at rates similar to those the country has experienced in the last two decades, the working-age population will decline by an additional 17.6 million people, further depressing the country's economic growth rate and its ability to support the Medicare and Social Security programs upon which the recently retired Boomers will rely.[57]

Without a comprehensive reform of our immigration policies and/or a change in the nation's birth rate, an increase in productivity, the other determinate of economic growth, becomes the only strategy left to pursue to provide Americans with the type of income growth they experienced in the last century. Unfortunately, growth in productivity has increased at the historically-low rate of only 1% per year since 2000.[58] Though no consensus among economists has yet emerged on how to accelerate America's tepid level of productivity growth, nearly everyone agrees that accelerating innovation must be a key part of the solution.

---

56 Sharma, R., *Why Trump Can't Make it 1981 Again,* New York Times, January 14, 2017

57 Passel, J.S. and Cohn, D., *Immigration Projected to Drive growth in U.S. working-age population through at least 2035,* Pew Research Center, March 8, 2017

58 DeLucia, R. F., Economic Perspective Newsletter, Nov. 13, 2017

In the five years after the Great Recession however, innovation, as measured by new business startups, dropped dramatically.[59] There was a net increase of only 104,600 new firms nationwide from 2010-2014, compared to close to one-half million from 1983 to 1987. Fortunately, starting in 2015, the Kaufman Index of startup activity reversed its direction and started heading upward again, just as median incomes and family's net worth also began to rise.

Republicans would argue that this slower growth in innovation and new business startups was due to the increased regulatory burden imposed by the Obama administration as part of its campaign to reform the financial services industry and to deal with climate change. The undoing of these regulations by the Trump administration will certainly put that theory to the test. Democrats are more likely to cite a reduction in appropriations for government-sponsored basic research as the reason for this decline. But these partisan arguments are, at most, limited answers to the challenge of how best to accelerate the innovation needed now to help increase economic opportunity for all Americans; and neither explains why the trend reversed itself in the final two years of the Obama administration.

Unfortunately for politicians in both parties, the economic rules of industrial economies that narrowed policy debates in the twentieth century to discussions about demand creation or supply management are of diminishing help in providing answers to the challenge of increasing innovation, and thereby productivity, in this century.

Today's debates by economists about what role the federal government should play to accelerate economic growth and more equitably allocate the fruits of that growth are being informed by insights from other disciplines, such as complexity theory and evolutionary biology. These new ideas, based on the notion that in an information-age economy innovation is the source of wealth because of the gains in productivity that flow from it, provide insights on how to address today's economic challenges. Instead of focusing on the federal government and its role in managing the economy, as economists have done since the New Deal, the new theories focus on encouraging innovation at the local level.[60] Indeed, data indicate that since the Great Reces-

---

59 *Dynamism in Retreat: Consequences for Regions, Markets, and Workers,* Economic Innovation Group

60 Beinhocker, E., *Origin of Wealth,* Harvard Business School Press, 2006

sion many of the nation's largest cities and metropolitan areas have emerged as the engines of U.S. innovation and growth, by creating environments that foster the birth of new ideas and companies.[61]

Economic theories supporting a move away from federal economic management to a focus on cities and metropolitan areas see innovation and economic growth as products of an economic ecosystem where a thousand flowers should bloom. The federal government has a continuing role to play in this new world through investments in basic research and education that serve as the fertilizer in emerging local economic hothouses. But government, in this alternative economic approach shouldn't attempt to dictate which of the new ideas that sprout should be given special treatment, nor should it try to protect existing structures from the threat of new competition. Rather, each innovation should be permitted to adapt to its environment through trial and error in order to determine its viability.[62] To foster experimentation and innovation in this new economic ecosystem existing safety nets should serve more as trampolines, providing the opportunity for failures to be followed by successes. Governments, particularly at the local level, should supply innovators and workers with a minimum level of support in the short run, while holding them accountable for their own independent performance in the long run.

Although the debate is not yet settled about precisely what economic theories offer the best strategies for accelerating innovation and productivity, increasingly, economists of all stripes agree that the long-term health of a knowledge economy requires a constant flow of new ideas and people, generated from free trade, immigration, and better-educated generations of young people. However, sharply-divided public opinion over the value of trade and immigration and the amount of support education should receive from the federal government, has prevented action at the national level on these issues, deepening frustration with Washington and stymying the adoption of policies that are essential for a vigorous information economy.

Globalization is a natural and desired outcome of an economic ecosystem built upon the value of information--the more of it the better. Facebook is the most valuable social media platform because of the number of people around the world who use it. Google's search engine draws more advertisers than any other because it is used by many more people.

---

61 Katz, B. and Bradley, J. *The Metropolitan Revolution*, Brookings Institutional Press, 2013

62 Liu, E. and Hanauer. N., *Gardens of Democracy*, Sasquatch Books, 2011

Unlike industrial economies, with their emphasis on maximizing the value of a country's natural resources and protecting domestic manufacturing firms from external competition, information economies grow best the more their products and services are shared.

Policies that limit global trade out of an understandable concern for the welfare of a country's workers and businesses impacted by the resulting redistribution of wealth and disruptive competition inevitably cripple the ability of that country to compete in the long run, making the future even worse for working families and their children. Instead of attempting to hold back the tide of a rising level of information-sharing and global economic growth, governments need to adopt policies that help those impacted by the flood to recover and build a new foundation for their successes on higher ground.

In such a world, the economic prospects of individual Americans are tied increasingly to their level of education. Of the fifteen states with the highest per capita income, three are energy-rich states. The other twelve, however, rank among the top fifteen states because of the average educational attainment of their citizens.[63] This is hardly surprising in a knowledge-based, innovation-driven economy. The same link between education and economic success is evident at the individual level. Just under half of those born in the early 1980s have been able to do as well as their parents, but 80% of those in that age category who have a college degree have managed to keep pace with, or exceed, their parents' standards of living.[64]

The share of jobs paying a minimum of $35,000 per year that don't require a four-year degree declined from about 60% of all workers in 1991, to 45% in 2015. Meanwhile, the need for higher skills has caused the minimal requirements for good-paying jobs to increase from having a high school education to getting a skills certificate at a technical college, or obtaining at least an associate's degree, which requires completing two years of study at a community college. Since the Great Recession of 2007-2009, more than twice as many new jobs were added to the economy for those with a four-year college degree (8.4 million) than for those with lesser levels of education (3.2 million).[65] Fewer than 100,000 net new jobs were created for those with

63 *2011-2015 American Community Survey 5-Year Estimates, Educational Attainment,* American Community Survey

64 *The AHCA Continuous Coverage Penalty and Young Adult Coverage,* Young Invincibles, March 2017

65 *Good Jobs that Pay Without a BA,* Georgetown University Center on Education and the

a high school degree or less. Like primary, and secondary education before it, higher education has become an essential public good for a community's economic development, as well as the key to increasing individual opportunity.

In summary, a central cause of American discontent with the performance of the economy and the failure of the federal government to accelerate economic and wage growth is that the nature of the American economy has changed dramatically since the New Deal, but its economic policies have not. What worked so well in the industrialized economy of the post-World War II years has lost much of its power to develop a strong economy in the information age. Furthermore, economic policies that economists agree promote innovation and increase productivity such as continued immigration and free trade currently lack the national public support required for federal action. Until our economic policies are built on these new insights about the workings of an evolving information economy and unless we find a way to take effective action in the absence of a national consensus, trust in the federal government to manage the American economy will continue to decline, draining confidence in our democratic system. Any new civic ethos must confront these challenges of both economic change and the lack of a national consensus to deal with the problem.

THERE IS NO INVISIBLE HAND TO HEAL US

Even when commentators concede that our current political, demographic, economic, and cultural divisions and unease reflect the impact of these changes and their underlying causes, there remains the hope that a political "invisible hand" is at work that will produce a solution that makes the problem magically disappear. Many on both sides of the partisan divide fantasize about how they might vanquish their opponents without having to give up any of their own policies or ideas for solving the real problems that confront our country. If they are correct, our current divisions will dissipate over time without the need for urgent public action or changes in our long-term strategy, and with no need for a new civic ethos.

Republicans are apt to plan for a day when Democrats and their New Deal approach are kicked to the dustbin of history by an electorate ineluctably moving to the Right. Democrats, on the other hand, are inclined to hope that as older generations, that are more likely to identify with and vote for Republicans, eventually die off and are replaced by younger generations that tend to identify with and vote for Democrats, politics and government will move in a liberal direction. There are historical precedents for both these political solutions, but neither is likely to happen in our lifetimes.

It is true, historically, that major American political parties have occasionally been displaced. The disappearance of the Federalist Party in the earliest years of the nineteenth century, as the nation was swept up in what was termed, an "era of good feelings," left the Democratic-Republican Party with a virtual monopoly of public support for a couple of decades, until the 1828 election of President Andrew Jackson and his rabble-rousing followers upset the establishment that opposed him. In roughly the same time period, the Whig Party came into being in opposition to Jacksonian Democrats; but it later dissolved into competing factions over the issues of race, trade protection, and immigration, eerily similar to today's intraparty divisions.

Other protest parties have arisen since the demise of the Whigs—the Populists in the last decades of the nineteenth century, Robert La Follette's Progressives in the 1920s, George Wallace's American Independents in 1968, and Ross Perot's Independent and Reform Party organizations in 1992 and 1996 among them—but none came close to replacing one of the major parties. Perhaps this is because Democrats and Republicans are better insulated from outside competition today than were the parties of the 1820s and 1850s.[66]

That is, In part, because the divisions between the parties today are far greater than the divisions within them, minimizing the opportunity to create a new party from factions of the existing ones.[67] Moreover, in an age of cable news networks, with each outlet using partisan bias to attract viewers in the same way newspapers did one hundred and fifty years ago to attract readers, air time is almost totally devoted to the two existing parties, leaving little room for alternative voices or parties to be heard, except on the fringes of the Internet. For better or worse, American politics is stuck with the two parties it has now, for at least the near term. Proposed solutions to our civic discontent must take this fact into account.

---

66 Wallach, P.A., *Prospects for Partisan Realignment: Lessons from the Demise of the Whigs,* Brookings Institution, March 6, 2017

67 *2014 Political Polarization Survey, Table 1.1: Ideological Consistency,* Pew Research Center, June 12, 2014

There also are examples of generational change impacting the country's political dynamics. The establishment of the New Deal civic ethos was enabled by a large influx of young GI Generation citizens who voted overwhelmingly (85%) for FDR in 1932, and who continued to vote Democratic for the rest of their lives, up to and including those who cast a majority of their votes for John Kerry in 2004.[68] The enthusiasm for President Reagan among members of Generation X who came of age at the time of his administration led to the creation of a core of GOP supporters, who have been unshakeable in their belief that, to quote their hero, "government is the problem, not the solution."[69] Indeed, some of those members of Generation X now make up the bulk of the current Republican leadership in the House of Representatives.

Although it is true that the Millennial generation's size and fondness for Democratic policies make the "just wait until they die off" scenario plausible for the ascendency of that side of today's political divide, there is no assurance that this gambit will work and it doesn't provide any immediate remedies for the current crisis in our nation's civic life.

Even though it might be comforting and easier to look to partisan capitulation or generational change to solve our governing problems and citizen loss of faith in our public institutions, right now there is no avoiding the need to tackle the economic, cultural, and demographic causes of our discontent head on. The country has pressing problems that need to be solved with sufficiently-broad support to be sustained long enough to be effective. If more and more people believe that the government doesn't work or, more malevolently, is rigged against them, they may turn to more extreme solutions—ones that may not respect constitutional rights and the rule of law. Dysfunctional democracy is the greatest threat to preserving our democracy, and fixing it is the most urgent task that those of us in public life should undertake.

It is past time for America to abandon its divisive debates about the efficacy and value of our current New Deal civic ethos and to create a new one that will demonstrate to a skeptical public that democracy can still solve their problems. The test of any proposed new civic ethos should be that it fully addresses the underlying causes of the dramatic changes we have experienced in this century.

---

68 Winograd, M. and Hais, M.D., *Millennial Makeover,* Rutgers University Press, 2008

69 *A Different Look at Generations and Partisanship,* Pew Research Center, April 30, 2015

We believe a shift to a governance system of Constitutional Localism has the ability to meet this test, address the country's discontents, and contribute significantly to healing our democracy.

CHAPTER FOUR:
CONSTITUTIONAL LOCALISM IS HOW TO HEAL DEMOCRACY IN A DIVIDED NATION

It has been said that the clearest sign that a paradigm has become obsolete is when what is most important to accomplish becomes impossible to get done. When the laissez-faire doctrine of government taking little, if any, role in the nation's business failed to prevent the ravages of the Great Depression, a majority of Americans were persuaded to look to the federal government to solve the big problems in their lives; and the New Deal was born. For a third of a century, it fulfilled its promise—providing Depression relief, Social Security, victory in World War II, the post-war economic boom, the long-awaited fulfillment of the promise of civil rights first made during Reconstruction, Medicare, and the successful defense of American values and interests in the Cold War.

Today, the perception of most Americans is that the national government cannot solve our most pressing problems. In this case, reality and perception are one. Rather than being a powerhouse of innovation and action, the federal government has descended into a paralysis that sustains an unsatisfactory status quo. Americans are looking for a new paradigm for how government should operate.

As we argued in Chapter Three, the hope that one group of partisans prevailing over the other side in the next election will provide the answer to this federal dysfunction is an illusion; if that were the way forward, it would have happened already. So far in the twenty-first century, each party has won the presidency several times only to be stymied by massive swings in Congressional control in the elections that followed. As a result, the country remains divided with no resolution to its problems in sight. Bipartisan calls to "come together" ring hollow given the deep partisan, demographic, cultural, and economic divisions among multiple groups of Americans. The old paradigm cannot be resurrected. It's time for a new one.

CONSTITUTIONAL LOCALISM DEFINED

To restore Americans' faith in their democracy, we offer a new civic paradigm— Constitutional Localism. "Localism", as we define it, seeks to acknowledge and reinforce what is already happening in the civic arena: Americans are increasingly looking away from Washington, not just to the states, but to their local communities and regions as more promising venues to solve common problems. Democratically debating and resolving public issues locally reduces the need to find answers that fit all communities across the country, thus making consensus easier to achieve. Solutions that are tailor-made to specific local circumstances make them more powerful. Democratic participation is more direct in a system of Constitutional Localism, thereby decreasing the chances of deadlock over distrust and differences in values. Furthermore, as we will argue in Chapter Five, the nature of many of our most urgent challenges, such as economic innovation, lend themselves best to local solutions.

Substantial majorities of Americans now believe that progress is more likely to occur in their hometowns and state capitals than in Washington.[70] Restoring faith in democracy requires people to experience some democratic successes, and these are most likely to occur at the local level. De Tocqueville recognized the invigorating impact of citizen participation at the local level 175 years ago writing: "Municipal institutions constitute the strength of free nations... A nation may establish a system of free government, but without the spirit of municipal institutions it cannot have the spirit of liberty."[71]

Most political discourse today focuses on our nation's divisions. Another way to regard the same phenomenon is to view the growing differences in personal lifestyle and public preferences as desirable diversity—greater freedom for Americans as individuals and as members of groups to live the way they want. Waiting for the country to return to the greater conformity that marked the Post-War era with three TV networks and a handful of national news magazines in an age of social media is a fanciful idea, not to mention contrary to what most Americans appear to prefer. Constitutional Localism, in short, is an approach to governance that seeks to preserve self-government in an increasingly diverse social and economic setting.

---

70 AllState/National Journal Heartland Monitor Poll XXII, February 22, 2015

71 Clark, C. and Teachout, W., *Slow Democracy: Rediscovering Community, Bring Decision Making Back Home,* Chelsea Green Publishing, 2012

Obviously, many decisions must remain at the national level, such as foreign policy and defense, as well as those commercial and environmental issues involving externalities that cross national and state lines or offer large economies of scale. However, more of the big issues facing Americans can be tackled at the local level than is commonly thought, including some of the most contentious, such as immigration, education, and policing.

The "Constitutional" dimension of our proposed new civic ethos provides both the essential boundaries within which local democratic decisions must occur as well as the ideas and values that can bind us together as one nation, even as we continue to disagree on matters of cultural and economic preference.

Like earlier answers to the question of what the scope and size of the federal government should be, this proposed new civic ethos begins with the Constitution of the United States and the Bill of Rights as a constant feature of American democracy. The Constitution, as it exists today or as amended in the future, must be recognized as establishing the framework for acceptable behavior by all levels of government for a system of localism to work. It is the only way we can ensure adherence to the "American Ideal", the set of principles of individual freedom and effective collective action that, along with the values expressed in our Declaration of Independence, have been the common bond that allowed a country with wide variations in its citizens' heritage and culture to unite as one democratic nation.

Only when that common commitment was abandoned has the future of the country been in jeopardy. Although local and state governments may want to test these boundaries from time to time, based on pressure from their constituents, for Constitutional Localism to work, the judicial system capped by the Supreme Court must stand as an unquestioned bulwark against any and all assaults on the constitutional rights and protections enshrined in our founding documents.

The "localism" dimension of our proposed new civic ethos reflects our belief that those who live in a community are the ones most likely to know what is best for it. Given the enormous variations in American life today, it is hard to conceive of any other governing principle that is more likely to produce both popular and effective solutions. Empowering local governments to tackle as broad a range of civic challenges as they are willing and able to undertake, within constitutional boundaries, should channel the energy of those who want to get further engaged in politics and government into the forum where it is most likely to produce results. As we discuss in the next chapter, there are already plenty of examples of communities who have risen to the challenge and become "laboratories of democracy," developing solutions that other communities, and even some states, have copied. Now we need a civic ethos that turns those examples into models for how we go about solving our problems as a matter of practice and preference.

We argue that Constitutional Localism, by shifting more public decision-making to the community level, is more than just an expedient way to temporarily escape the enervating and potentially democracy-threatening deadlock in Washington, though we believe that this is an important near-term payoff for a country in urgent need of renewed confidence in democratic governance. We also advocate for it as a fundamental democratic adaptation for Americans who increasingly expect to be able to choose from among different social mores, life styles, political philosophies, and economic opportunities without sacrificing either self-government or membership in a great nation. Bringing decisions involving both common opportunities and responsibilities closer to home satisfies the first desire, while insisting on the preservation of the ideas that unify us as Americans, such as individual freedom, self-government, rule of law, and the preservation of basic individual rights against the tyranny of the majority, provide the path to the second.

Over the past half-century, democratic participation has ebbed as more and more meaningful public decisions played out in Washington or distant state capitals. A return to community decision-making offers the opportunity to make democratic governance personal again.

"LOCALISM" IS A POPULAR IDEA

Americans already believe that local governance, rather than Washington, offers the best hope going forward.

In 1958, about three-quarters of Americans (73%) believed that the national government could be counted on to do the right thing "just about always" or "most of the time." The level of trust rose to nearly eight-in-ten in 1964, but within a decade, as a result of the Vietnam War, civil unrest, and the Watergate scandal, it fell to just over one in three (36%). By the end of the 1970s, only a quarter of Americans believed they could trust the federal government at least most of the time. And, according to Pew, "Since July

2007, the share saying they can trust the federal government has generally fluctuated in a narrow range, between 20% and 25%." That number was 19% in a Pew 2015 survey[72] and rose no higher in the early months of the Trump presidency.[73]

Although most Americans now have negative attitudes toward the federal government, they are not inherently opposed to any and all government. The 2015 Pew survey asked respondents if they "have a favorable view" of the federal government and their state and local governments. Thirty-two percent of Americans were positive about the federal government. By contrast, majorities were favorable toward both state (56%) and local government (65%). While Democrats and Republicans disagreed on how they felt about the government in Washington, majorities of partisans from both parties were favorable toward both state and local government. Finally, while attitudes toward the federal and, to a lesser extent, state governments varied over time depending on factors like the party affiliations of chief executives in Washington and state capitals; perceptions of local government were stable. In a series of more than a dozen Pew surveys conducted since 1997, two-thirds of Americans consistently had positive perceptions of their local governments.[74]

A Heartland Monitor poll fielded in 2015 had similar results. In that survey, two-thirds (66%) perceived their local area was moving in the right direction; only half that percentage believed the same about the country. Even as President Obama's performance evaluation was evenly split (46% approve vs. 48% disapprove) and that of Congress was overwhelmingly negative (18% approve vs. 71% disapprove), 60% approved of the job "political leaders in their local area" were doing.[75]

It might be argued that the reason Americans are favorable about their local governments is that those governments provide benign and non-controversial services, such as fire protection, trash collection, libraries and parks. But, local governments also take the lead in delivering public policing and primary and secondary education services. And they provide a portion of

---

72 *Public Trust in Government, 1958-2017*, Pew Research Center, May 3, 2017

73 *Public Trust in Government Remains Near Historic Lows as Partisan Attitudes Shift,* Pew Research Center, May 3, 2017

74 *Beyond Distrust: How Americans View Their Government, 4. Ratings of Federal Agencies, Congress, and the Supreme Court,* Pew Research Center, November 23, 2015

75 AllState/National Journal Heartland Monitor Poll XXII, February 22, 2015

the country's healthcare services. All of these topics are the focus of frequent and rancorous ideological debates. Nevertheless, attitudes toward local governments remain consistently positive.

A series of Heartland Monitor surveys begun in 2015 suggests a reason why local governments are the most popular layer of government in our federal system. They showed that a large majority of Americans perceived that progress dealing with the range of major issues confronting and vexing the United States is occurring more often at the state and local level (64%) than in Washington (26%). An even greater percentage (69%) expect that in the future "new ideas and solutions for the biggest economic and social challenges facing America" are more likely to come from "state and local institutions like government, businesses, and volunteer or community organizations," rather than similar national institutions (22%). The public believes that institutions nearer to home will do better in resolving issues because they are "closer to the problems, more adaptable, and have more at stake in finding solutions," even if they might have fewer "financial resources," and less "experience" and "long-term stability" than national institutions.[76] A year later, by a virtually identical 68% to 23% margin, Americans again expected state and local, rather than national institutions, to be the most likely sources of solutions to the country's challenges.[77]

This perception crossed demographic and partisan lines. The same surveys revealed that the belief that "new ideas for confronting the nation's biggest problems were more likely to emerge from state and local institutions than national ones...was shared by two-thirds of whites and nonwhites, and at least two-thirds of Millennials, Generation X'ers, and Baby Boomers. At 59%, the oldest respondents were only slightly less likely to lean that way." In addition, "Nearly four-fifths of Trump supporters thought local institutions offered the best new thinking, and although Clinton supporters tilted more toward Washington, nearly three-fifths of them as well looked local for answers."[78]

But, if there was a single survey question demonstrating that Americans feel that progress will come from their local areas and communities, rather than from a partisan victory in Washington, it was one asked in the

---

76 Ibid

77 All State/National Journal Heartland Poll XXVI, June 30, 2016

78 Brownstein, R., *Why Americans Argue Nationally but Act Locally,* Atlantic, July 12, 2016

Heartland Monitor poll a few months before the 2016 election. Nearly half (47%) indicated they believed that the greatest progress would come from "positive actions taken by some combination of businesses, local governments, non-profits, and Americans themselves." A quarter (26%) said it would most likely result from "Individuals taking action in their communities." Just one-in-five (22%) believed that progress would most likely occur by "electing a president you mostly agree with on the issues."[79]

Again, this perception was widespread. According to Ron Brownstein, "Trump supporters (29%) were only slightly more likely than Clinton backers (23%) to say that electing a president they agreed with was most likely to produce progress. Nearly three-fourths of Clinton's supporters and almost two-thirds of Trump's, said actions by local institutions or individuals were most likely to generate gains."[80]

So, despite yawning cultural, economic, and partisan differences, Americans by substantial majorities believe that their localities offer the best opportunity to find common ground regarding public challenges and opportunities.

CONSTITUTIONAL PROTECTIONS IN AN ERA OF INCREASED LOCALISM

The fear that shifting to a civic ethos that moves the maximum number of public decisions to the community level will give free reign to local prejudices that threaten individual rights, especially those of local minorities, is understandable given our country's history. However, we believe that a civic ethos emphasizing the empowerment of local governments can avoid this danger if it is sufficiently grounded in Constitutional principles. State governments already operate under a system of givens and constraints when it comes to their relationship with the federal government. Under Constitutional Localism, state governments also would have to enter an analogous relationship with their local governments. They cannot be prohibited, of course, from attempting to define acceptable behavior by their local governments, but Constitutional Localism's purpose is to let the relative homogeneity of counties, cities, towns, or even villages provide opportunities for innovation and consensus-building. Even in localities that reflect the broader diversity

---

79 AllState/National Journal Heartland Monitor Poll XXVI, June 24, 2016

80 Brownstein, R., *Why Americans Argue Nationally but Act Locally,* Atlantic, July 12, 2016

of the country, smaller, more personal venues create a climate where civil discussion and collaborative decision-making is more likely. In this governing paradigm, states will be expected to exercise their inherent powers with a good deal of caution and self-imposed constraint.

For example, many states have incorporated prohibitions on discrimination by gender, either in their constitutions or by statute, even though the equal rights amendment to the U.S. Constitution has not been adopted. These states range from the very red, such as Alabama, to the very blue, such as California or Maryland, and every shade in between. In such states, under a Constitutional Localism framework, communities would not be permitted to adopt ordinances that would permit discriminatory behavior on the basis of gender, let alone encourage it. Meanwhile, those committed to banishing discrimination based on gender who don't live in such states could choose to get involved in creating such prohibitions at any level they felt most able to impact—their community, their state or even the federal government. When rights or practices are not embodied in federal or state constitutions or statutes, Constitutional Localism envisions each community deciding what policies, if any, it wishes to adopt for its citizens on these issues.

Placing power closest to the governing bodies Americans trust the most, and pay attention to the most, maximizes the chances that current constraints on individual freedoms will change more quickly in response to developments in the community, long before the more distant and diverse governmental entities at the state or even federal level feel compelled to adjust their own laws on such matters. This means accepting the notion that the community next door may deal with matters such as race, gender, or privacy in ways that are significantly different from the community one lives in, providing there is no constitutional prohibition from doing so.

If this understanding of the role of states versus their local communities had been in place, North Carolina might have avoided the disruptive and divisive debate over "who should use what bathroom" that contributed to Governor Pat McCrory's reelection loss in 2016, the first time in the state's history a governor failed to get reelected. By attempting to impose its ideas on transgender rights on every city in the state, the legislature's passage of SB2 robbed some communities of the ability to offer their transgendered citizens the right to use the public restroom of their choice. The Charlotte-Mecklenberg County's NAACP led the fight to repeal SB2 to preserve the power of the community to make this decision independent of any state mandate, even though the rights of the LGBTQ community had not traditionally been its central concern.

After the election was over and a Democratic governor had been sworn in, it still took two attempts to settle the issue. Each city, under the compromise passed by the Republican legislature at the urging of the new governor, was empowered to eventually make its own decision about who would be allowed to use what bathroom. Although that outcome didn't satisfy purists on either side of the issue, it did bring an end to the debate so that, even in this still highly-polarized and politically-divided state, the government could begin to function again. If a system of Constitutional Localism had been in place, the state would have arrived at the same solution from the start, without all the divisive debate that further inflamed their cultural divide.

States have also attempted to intervene in how local police departments work with federal forces charged with enforcing immigration laws. The Republican-dominated Texas legislature approved a sweeping prohibition on any city making itself a "sanctuary city," i.e. instructing its police department not to cooperate with federal authorities charged with enforcing immigration laws working in its community. As signed by the governor, the law threatens local law enforcement leaders with jail time if they fail to comply with the legislation's directives.

In direct contrast, the California legislature debated a law that dictated limits on how much cooperation its state's local police forces could provide to federal ICE agents. But California Governor Jerry Brown refused to support the legislation unless it made clear that immigration authorities could still work with personnel running the state's prisons and county jails. In addition, the proposed law created an exemption for otherwise-prohibited interactions between local police and ICE if the person involved had been convicted of a set of specified violent crimes or serious felonies. With these changes, the California Police Chiefs Association withdrew its opposition, even as the California State Sheriffs' Association remained in opposition, thus reflecting the differences in the communities the respective organizations' members patrol.

Neither of these debates would have taken place if the state governments involved could have resisted the temptation to intervene in what has traditionally been an inherently local matter, policing. By attempting to impose one set of values on the behavior of local officials whose constituents might have another set of beliefs, these state actions reinforced existing divisions and did nothing to bring unity of purpose to either state.

In summary, we believe a new civic ethos of Constitutional Localism replacing the New Deal's more centralized governing paradigm offers a framework that will restore Americans' confidence in democracy, while protecting the values and basic rights embedded in our founding documents that define us as Americans. Whether reorganizing governance in the country to shift more authority and responsibility to the local level in response to strong public preference effectively aligns this new civic ethos with the forces reshaping America will ultimately determine its success. In the short term, Constitutional Localism will only succeed if it can produce the results needed to restore faith in democratic governing processes in a timely fashion. In the next two chapters, we describe why and how we believe Constitutional Localism can meet both of these challenges.

CHAPTER FIVE:
HOW CONSTITUTIONAL LOCALISM FITS THE TIMES

While polls show strong public support for shifting more governing authority to the local level, we believe this emerging civic ethos also responds effectively to the forces that have disrupted the New Deal governing framework. Popularity is a good starting place, but Constitutional Localism should only be pursued if it allows the nation to deal successfully with the deep-seated economic and cultural concerns that are continuing to divide the country and damaging public confidence in our democratic system of government.

LOCALISM AND THE INFORMATION ECONOMY

Increasing American prosperity at a time of low birth rates and reduced immigration must rely on increased productivity through innovation to generate economic growth. Constitutional Localism seeks to address this challenge through systematic efforts to support decentralized approaches to the testing and implementing of new ideas, as well as providing communities and regions with the resources and autonomy to customize their economies in ways designed to maximize innovation.

An information age economy requires a continuous infusion of new ideas to fuel its growth. For much of the 20th Century, such new ideas were encouraged by the federal government, often with a military implication, through research funding from agencies such as the Defense Advanced Research Program Agency (DARPA) or the Department of Energy. Improvements in medical treatments were similarly focused on research funded by grants from federal agencies such as the National Institutes of Health to university-based researchers. These federal investments in R&D remain critical to our economic vitality. However, the economy needs many more ideas to grow than can emerge from such bureaucratically governed and politically dependent processes.

Fortunately, we are beginning to see local communities moving to fill that productivity gap by developing the specialized infrastructure and talent they need to become national and world-leading locations for different types of economic activity. Silicon Valley became a great local success story by embracing technologies to increase individual productivity in every phase of our lives. The Valley's civic leaders consciously focused on creating a collaborative, sharing ecosystem for scientists and entrepreneurs to take advantage of the high-powered research universities, both public and private, in their midst. As documented in Anna Lee Sexinen's book, *Regional Advantage: Culture and Competition in Silicon Valley and Route 128*, this nurturing of local innovation produced life-changing inventions for the entire world. The resulting wealth that flowed back to the region has helped fuel successive waves of economic growth for those individuals and communities most plugged into the innovation economy.

New Orleans offers a very different example of local decisions creating a competitive advantage for a community, in this case one that had been written off as economically moribund following Hurricane Katrina. As Joel Kotkin and Michael Lind documented, city leadership came together in the wake of the disaster and decided to strategically leverage "New Orleans' intrinsic strengths - its Mississippi River location, energy infrastructure, and world-famous culture - in order to diversify the economy and re-build the middle class." Industrial companies invested $70 billion in new projects. A former NASA factory, for example, was converted to the production of commercial drones and composite windmill blades. The result has been a steady influx of technology companies placing New Orleans second among all U.S. cities in the growth of "knowledge industries" and number one in the volume of in-migration of college graduates. Federal recovery capital played a significant role.

However, the "new New Orleans" that emerged from these efforts is mostly the product of local public-private partnerships that have combined to make the city the national leader in population growth since 2010.[81]

Accelerating productivity and ensuring it is broadly shared also demands innovation in the social sector that is often best achieved at the local level. Kalamazoo, Michigan offers a great example of this type of local innovation.

---

81 Kotkin, J. and Lind, M., *The New American Heartland: Renewing the Middle Class by Revitalizing Middle America, Center for Opportunity Urbanism*, Houston, 2017

Kalamazoo is a mid-sized community in the heart of the country's rust belt. None of its supposed constraints based on size or location prevented it from coming up with an idea that is revolutionizing higher education in America. In 2005, a small group of donors (who remain anonymous to this day) created the Kalamazoo Promise by making an extraordinary investment in the city's youth to improve both social and economic development in the city. By using its money to create a reason for people to live in, and hopefully move back to, the city, Kalamazoo hoped to create an ever-increasing tax base instead of having to raise rates to generate more revenue.

The Promise offered any graduate of the city's public schools free tuition at any of Michigan's colleges or universities, provided those students maintained a 2.0 grade point average and made progress toward a degree. (The idea has since been expended to include 15 private colleges in the state that were willing to accept public tuition levels for Promise students.) Scholarship levels varied based on how many grades the student attended in the city's public schools, not on a determination of need or merit. And so was born the first "place-based" scholarship program in the country.[82]

A study by the Upjohn Institute for Employment Research showed that ten years after the Promise was put into effect, students in the Kalamazoo Public Schools were graduating from high school, enrolling in college, and completing their studies at rates that exceeded their non-public school counterparts in every demographic category.[83]

The community's innovative idea, based on its knowledge of uniquely local conditions, worked. In the 20 years before the Promise Program was implemented, Kalamazoo was experiencing a steady population decline, stagnating wages, and high unemployment. In the years immediately following the implementation of the program, enrollment of local students in Kalamazoo Public Schools increased, and wages, salaries, and employment were the best of the 14 Metropolitan Statistical Areas in Michigan. The city's population also began to increase.[84] None of this would have happened without this type of social system innovation at the community level.

---

82 Winograd, M. and Hais, M.D., *Millennial Momentum*, Rutgers University Press, 2011

83 Bartik, T.J., Hersbein, B.J., and Lachowsak, M., The *Effects of the Kalamazoo Promise Scholarship on College Enrollment, Persistence, and Completion*, W.E. Upjohn Institute, 2015

84 *The Kalamazoo Promise, Freecollegenow.org*, 2016

Such local innovation is not limited to just education or economics. For example, almost every community now has some form of recycling initiative to save money as well as the environment. Unlike the emotional and hotly debated discussions of climate change at the federal level, these programs depend upon the commitment of its residents for their success and were adopted by each community with little disagreement. It is time to recognize and celebrate this trend toward increasingly effective local solutions by shifting resources and governing authority to communities, so they can more effectively lead the way.

GOVERNING SUCCESSES FOR A DIVERSE AMERICA

We believe that enough areas of American life, particularly those that most concern voters, can be shifted to local communities so those localities can deal with the challenges in ways that positively impact Americans' feelings about democratic governance. This is true for even such hot button issues as immigration and urban education.

Immigration emerged as a central issue in the 2016 Presidential race, one that divided the country deeply. Voters in many communities, especially in larger cities and more affluent suburbs, favored a continuing flow of immigrants into the U.S., while voters in smaller towns, exurbs, and rural areas often urged a reduction in immigration perceiving it as a threat to both American jobs and culture. Neither President Bush nor President Obama were able to forge a strong enough bipartisan consensus in Washington to build an immigration system for the 21st century despite16 years of committed efforts.

Even while agreeing with the courts and the Constitution that the basic rules for deciding who can immigrate to the US and the required application process are a matter for the federal government to decide, shifting a key element of the immigration question to the local level could open the door for action that recognizes these divergent views. Requiring that potential immigrants who have been federally vetted receive a community sponsorship before qualifying to enter the country would allow places like Detroit, Silicon Valley, and farm areas in rural Georgia that are hungry for immigrant workers to continue to welcome them into their respective communities. Such an approach would also permit rust-belt cities like Youngstown or small towns in Alabama to decline the initial placement of new immigrants in their communities, given their concern about possible higher unemployment or a desire for more cultural homogeneity. Of course, the Constitution would prohibit any restriction on the subsequent voluntary movement of immigrants once legally settled in their sponsoring communities, but under this plan each community would be more likely to feel its preferences had been respected. The result should be a better experience for new immigrants and a lessening of the divisiveness this issue continues to cause.

Another issue currently dividing the nation's Capital is how best to educate low-income and minority children. The often-acrimonious debate revolves around whether to increase school choice and tax credits for private and religious schools or to provide more resources for traditional public schools as the best way to restore education quality to the levels required for international competitiveness and economic prosperity. No Congressional bipartisan consensus is remotely in the offing based upon the highly emotional and closely decided debate in the U.S. Senate over confirming voucher-advocate Betsy DeVos as President Trump's Education Secretary.

Yet while all this sound and fury echoes across Washington, some communities have found a way forward. Denver is a good example. In 2005 the Denver Public Schools (DPS) had the lowest rate of academic growth among Colorado's ten largest school districts. There were 31,000 empty school seats out of a total of 98,000 and 16,000 students had left the system for private schools and neighboring public schools under the state's choice statute. These developments, along with problems funding the district's teachers' pension fund, put the district in financial peril.

But just seven years later, DPS could boast that it had the highest academic growth rate among the ten largest Colorado systems. The turnaround occurred despite the district's challenging demographics, which include nearly 70% low-income students (94% of whom are of color) and 37% English language learners. This dramatic reversal of fortunes was the result of inspired and persistent local efforts, not something imposed from on high. One hundred influential Denverites, led by two former mayors, created A+ Denver in 2006 to provide civic support for needed reforms. The new DPS Superintendent wrote that the "district should no longer function as a one-size-fits-all, centralized, industrial age enterprise making choices that schools, principals, teachers, and most, most important, parents are in a much better position to make for themselves."

The New School Development Plan they created offered existing schools more autonomy in return for accountability with consequences. Failing schools were replaced with new schools operated by whoever offered the most persuasive evidence of promised success. High performing charters were given opportunities to expand, while many traditional schools were granted more charter-like independence. It was and continues to be a messy process that constantly evolves, but it provided the kind of progress in educating Denver children that no federal or state policies have credibly produced on their own.[85]

The story from Denver and other cities such as Indianapolis, Washington D.C., and New Orleans, where public charter schools have educated low-income children of color at substantially higher levels of achievement than those communities' traditional public schools, is not simply that school choice by itself is the answer. Charter schools' edge in improving their students' education only appears in places where one or two public bodies manage the local education marketplace. Denver's outcomes are the result of the Denver Board of Education systematically closing low-performing charter schools quickly while supporting the expansion of charter organizations that are achieving the best results. In cities like Detroit, where no such market-managing body exists and virtually all the state's universities and local school districts can authorize charter schools, the performance gap between charters and traditional schools is smaller. These results suggest the need for new governance structures supported and encouraged at the state and federal levels that will examine the results of local experimentation and help spread those that prove effective, while weeding out those that don't. We will describe the best way to create such structures in the next chapter, but the evidence of their positive impact on improving K-12 educational performance underlines the importance of instituting new governance models to make Constitutional Localism work in America's increasingly diverse communities.

LOCALISM AND THE MILLENNIAL GENERATION

For Constitutional Localism or any other new civic ethos to succeed in the future, it must align with the values and beliefs of America's rising and largest generation, Millennials. Born between 1982 and 2003, the 92 million Millennials will soon comprise more than a third of U.S. adults, enabling them to dominate the U.S. electorate. Millennials are just beginning to run for public

85 Osborne, D., *Reinventing America's Schools: Creating a 21st Century Education System*, Bloomsbury USA, 2017

office and will form the core of community leadership for the next several decades. Unlike the constantly battling and divided Baby Boomer generation now in power, polls suggest Millennials bring a greater sense of unity, compromise and collaboration in their politics and community participation, something that will only enhance local activism.

Although, a majority of Millennials have identified with or leaned to the Democratic Party since Pew Research began measuring the generation's political attitudes in 2004, the generation is by no means monolithic in its political beliefs

Importantly, Republican Millennials, who represent about a third of the generation, are different from older Republicans because they are more moderate in their views.[86] A 2014 Pew study placed Republican and Democratic identifiers on an ideological scale based on their attitudes on social, racial, economic and foreign policy issues. A majority (53%) of all Republicans were classified as either "consistently" or "mostly" conservative. A similar majority (56%) of Democrats were classified as either "consistently" or "mostly" liberal. Partisans of all generations except for one—Republican Millennials—replicated this pattern. Only a third of that cohort expressed conservative attitudes, while 51% were moderate.

The moderation of Millennial Republicans is even clearer on specific issues, especially those dealing with the cultural matters that have deeply split the country in recent decades.

Almost two thirds (64%) of Republican Millennials think that "homosexuality should be accepted by society; 57% believe "immigrants strengthen our society"; and half agree "business corporations make too much profit. Almost the same percentage (48%), believe "stricter environmental laws and regulations are worth the cost." In fact, on all these issues Millennial Republicans are closer in their beliefs to their Democratic generational peers than to older Republicans. Only on matters of economic policy do Millennial Republicans resemble their partisan elders. The lack of sharp ideological differences on many issues among Millennials makes their generation a promising foundation on which to build a civic ethos based on local collaboration and inclusion.

---

86 *A Wider Partisan and Ideological Gap Between Younger, Older Generations,* Pew Research Center, March 20, 2017

Beyond this, there is evidence---quantitative and anecdotal---suggesting that Constitutional Localism would find favor with Millennials because it aligns with the generation's attitudes and behavior, especially its characteristic preference for thinking globally, while acting locally.[87] A large survey of Millennials by NBC News in partnership with GenForward taken at the beginning of 2018 found that three-quarters of those interviewed thought the efforts of organizations and groups working in communities could be effective in producing real change in the country.[88]

These beliefs are translated into action across the country every day by members of this generation. For instance, a group of Millennials in San Bernardino, California decided to deal directly with the economic and governmental decline of their city, not by appealing for more money from federal or state governments, but by taking action on their own at the local level.

They formed San Bernardino Generation Now, "an interesting cocktail of civic engagement and community involvement with politics mixed in." Michael Segura, one of Generation Now's founders, believes "Local is where it really matters." Similarly, Jorge Heredia, the group's civic action committee leader, stated that the group is about "encouraging people to be part of the [civic] conversation because politicians only serve active people." Summing it up neatly, another group member said that, "We have to be the ones to step up even though we're young."

On the East Coast, in Bridgeport, Connecticut, a city with economic and governmental concerns like those of San Bernardino, another Millennial, Calabria Gale Heilmann, was inspired by the community-based example of the California organization. She and a group of friends established BPT Generation Now, "to boost civic engagement and create a new cultural identity for Bridgeport."

The two Generation Now organizations share a name and the goals of transforming a community by giving Millennials a voice in shaping the future. But, both groups are truly local and have not adopted a one-size-fits-all approach. San Bernardino Generation Now was set up as a social club rather than a nonprofit so it could be politically active. BPT Generation Now regis-

---

87 Rynne, A., *Millennial Minute: The Global Emergence of Socially Conscious Consumers*, LinkedIn Marketing Solutions Blog, July 12, 2016

88 Perry, S. and Arenge. A., *https://www.nbcnews.com/politics/politics-news/poll-millennialssay-country-wrong-track-they-re-not-n841526*, January 29, 2018

tered as a nonprofit so it could apply for grants and offer tax-deductible status to donors and members, an approach Heilmann said is the "right fit for us at this point of our existence."[89]

Whether or not either of these efforts succeeds in transforming their community remains to be seen, but the attitudes and actions of those involved in the two "Now" organizations help illustrate why Constitutional Localism is likely to be a good fit with the rising Millennial generation.

Millennials believe this type of local action is a more effective way to change things in comparison to participating in elections. The NBC/GenForward survey gave the nod to community group action over elections by a 22 point margin (75% to 53%).[90] The Case Foundation's longitudinal research examined the cause-oriented and philanthropic activities of Millennials and found that Millennials' overall interest in the election was superficial. Over the course of the 2016 campaign an ever-larger share of the cohort soured on the efficacy of participating in the traditional political process. The percentage believing that they could make the country better dropped while the number saying that they didn't want to vote for either major party candidate or that they had a "neutral" political ideology rose.[91]

However, the same research did not find that the Millennial generation was apathetic when it came to civic engagement As Elizabeth Matto, a professor who heads the Rutgers University Youth Political Participation Program, explains, "Students think of politics as something that takes place in D.C. or the presidential campaign, when most of our everyday lives (sic) is affected by what's going on in your city council or your board of education." Since 2010, Case research has demonstrated that "with few exceptions, Millennials [are] willing and eager to 'do good'." But, rather than attempting to make things better through large organizations and institutions, Case surveys indicate that Millennials prefer to support specific issues and perform smaller actions locally, often as volunteers utilizing non-governmental channels.[92]

---

89 *Meet the Millennials Who Hope to Improve Southern California,* The Press-Enterprise, January 20, 2017

90 Perry, S. and Arenge. A., *https://www.nbcnews.com/politics/politics-news/poll-millennialssay-country-wrong-track-they-re-not-n841526,* January 29, 2018

91 *The Millennial Impact Report,* Case Foundation, 2016

92 Feldmann, D. *A Generation for Causes: A Four-Year Summary of the Millennial Impact Project,* Case Foundation, 2015

A 2016 post-election poll analysis by CIRCLE, an organization that researches and promotes youth civic engagement, provides additional survey evidence of the substantial local community involvement of Millennials and their preference for such actions rather than conventional political participation. The CIRCLE survey asked its sample of Millennials if they had ever performed an array of specific political and civic activities. The study indicated that three-quarters of Millennials had voted in a local election, half had donated money to a cause, and a third volunteered for a community organization on a regular basis. Between a fifth and a quarter had contacted a public official about local issues, attended a meeting to discuss local issues, and served in a leadership role in a community organization. Twice those numbers said they would participate in those activities if they had an opportunity to do so. By contrast, only about one-in-ten Millennials said they had ever volunteered for or donated money to a political campaign or had attended a campaign rally or event.[93]

The Millennial generation will soon dominate the nation's electorate and provide the bulk of its governmental and civic leadership. Because Constitutional Localism comports so well with the values of Millennials and the way in which they prefer to engage in civic matters, we believe it provides a political and governmental framework that will effectively harness the potential of this soon-to-be dominant force in America's civic life. In so doing, it should help to make progress on the deep-seated issues that have vexed and divided the United States for years and restore public faith in our civic institutions.

But, to do so effectively requires a mechanism for sharing the policies that have proven to be successful in one locality for others to replicate. Fortunately, Millennials' obsessions with sharing and social media should make this new, critical task of Constitutional Localism much easier to implement and more likely to succeed than in the past.

---

93 *Millennials After 2016: A Post-Election Poll Analysis,* The Center for Information and Research on Civic Learning and Engagement, 2016

CHAPTER SIX:
MAKING CONSTITUTIONAL LOCALISM
A GAME CHANGER

For all the reasons enumerated in the previous chapter, we believe the promise of effective community problem-solving should make Constitutional Localism inherently attractive to those interested in improving civic life in America. However, if Constitutional Localism is to fulfill its promise of restoring faith in American democracy through experiential learning, it is not enough for individual communities to successfully solve their local problems. Although to do so would have enormous benefit for those communities and the individuals involved, new ideas and solutions will still need to spread from one community to others that share similar challenges and circumstances. If Constitutional Localism is to have an impact on the nation as a whole, there must be ways to ensure that the best ideas emerge from this hoped-for hothouse of local experimentation and spread rapidly across the country.

Over the years, the U.S. has developed communication and social linkages between states and from states to the federal government on public policy issues, but the infrastructure for sharing ideas among localities will need to become much more robust if Constitutional Localism is to succeed. The Ash Center for Democratic Governance and Innovation at Harvard's Kennedy School has taken the lead in promoting the sharing of good ideas between local communities.[94] Unfortunately, its Project on Municipal Innovation is one of only two platforms that cities can use to share and adapt best practices and innovative policy ideas. The other, the Knowledge Network, sponsored by the International City/County Managers Association (ICMA), provides city managers and other municipal staff information on how other communities have dealt with a comprehensive range of issues, but it does not involve elected officials in their work.[95] For Constitutional Localism to achieve

---

94 *https://ash.harvard.edu/local-innovation*

95 *https://icma.org/*

the scale needed to restore trust in our democratic institutions and address the crisis of confidence in our civic life, a comprehensive system for moving ideas from community to community and up and down the ladder of our federal system, using the very latest in communication and computer technologies, must be built upon the pioneering efforts already in place.

AN IMPROVISED EXAMPLE OF SHARING A DREAM

In his treatise, *Diffusion of Innovation*, political scientist, Everett Rogers, identified several elements necessary for a truly innovative idea to spread.[96] These are (1) a *communication system* to disseminate information about the idea to other individuals and groups, (2) a *social system* that contains communities of practitioners who are interested in and capable of attempting to replicate the idea, and (3) *time* for the idea to gain adoption within those social systems. The growth of Promise Programs from the initial experiment in Kalamazoo, in 2005, to its implementation in over two hundred local communities and ten states twelve years later, provides validation of Rogers' theory. It also offers insights on how to systematically spread ideas in an Internet-driven age.

When the Kalamazoo Promise was launched in 2005, it was the first "place-based scholarship" program in the country. Fortunately, the visionaries who created it also invested time and energy in sharing their new idea with communities and states across America. This provided a model that others could utilize to systematically communicate their own great community public policies.

At the time it was written, Rogers' book identified only two communication systems—mass media and interpersonal communications—for spreading information about new ideas. The leading researcher on Promise Programs, Michelle Miller-Adams, who was there at the beginning of the Kalamazoo Promise, identified both channels as important in the spread of the idea of place-based scholarships immediately after the local Promise was announced.[97]

The Kalamazoo Promise was the subject of numerous national news

---

96 Rogers, E., *Diffusion of Innovations, 5th Edition,* Free Press: 2003

97 Miller-Adams, M., *The Kalamazoo Promise and the Diffusion of a Private Policy Innovation,* 2009

stories from its inception, which generated a large number of requests from local communities for more information about the program. In order to organize a response to those requests, the W.E. Upjohn Institute for Employment Research gathered the leaders of the Promise Program to discuss the possibility of convening a conference about the idea. Using only the lists of those who had inquired about the Kalamazoo Promise, the planning group was able to bring more than two hundred people together in June 2008 for the first PromiseNet conference, thereby establishing the type of interpersonal communications Rogers suggests is needed for innovation diffusion to take place. The conference planners deliberately created a mutual learning experience, rather than the usual PowerPoint lectures from experts, a format that has been used in each annual gathering since. Within eight years, the PromiseNet conference had grown to an event that filled the halls of the Washington Convention Center, with participants treated to White House briefings and a reception hosted by Vice President and Dr. Jill Biden at their home.

As impressive as this effort to use interpersonal communications was, it pales in comparison to what will be needed to spread other equally innovative ideas from communities throughout the country, at the speed necessary to impact our current civic crisis. Now, however, there is an important additional communication channel--social media platforms on the Internet-- that wasn't available when the Kalamazoo Promise was launched. Still, even back then, the Upjohn Institute recognized the power of websites that were rapidly populating the Internet to spread awareness of the Program and its results. It established a section on its website about the Promise that was being downloaded at the rate of 2000 to 3000 per month within a year of the Program's inception. However, the information provided was often too theoretical and in a format that made it difficult to use by some of the communities just starting promise initiatives of their own.

So, when attendees at the 2014 PromiseNet conference were asked what more they needed from the organizers to help them with their own plans for initiating Promise Programs, the most frequent request was for a better website where information about all Promise Programs, not just Kalamazoo's, would be available. In response to this request, several new websites were created that presented the information with user-friendly graphics, including a national map showing what communities had initiated Promise Programs and the status of those individual programs. One of those sites, freecollegenow.org, was generating up to 3000 views per week by 2017. Fittingly, in the emerging Internet-based era, the same delegates soundly rejected the idea of forming an academic center to provide top down direction for the evolution of Promise Programs.

Since 2005 when the Kalamazoo Promise was launched the availability of more powerful Internet searching capabilities, coupled with the capability of social media to reinforce interest in any topic with continuing conversations and discussions, has created a third communication channel that must be a part of any systematic effort to share and replicate the solutions that emerge from community-based "laboratories of democracy." Using such channels for sharing ideas that work offers a way to use social media to create connections across communities and among individuals. In direct contrast to criticisms of social media for its tendency to allow people to retreat into their own ideological silos and shut out information about what else is going on in the world around them, properly designed and implemented, social media networks can provide the technological underpinnings for the spread of Constitutional Localism across the country.

MOVING SUCCESSFUL SOLUTIONS UP AND DOWN THE FEDERAL LADDER

The history of the diffusion of the Kalamazoo Promise from a city in Michigan, to the state of Tennessee to a topic of national policy debates also offers insight into how Constitutional Localism can spark the large-scale transfer of local successes up and down the layers of our federal system.

In 2008, the Knox County, Tennessee "Mayor" or chief executive, Mike Ragsdale, was lobbied by his neighbor, Randy Boyd, a very successful entrepreneur and dog lover, to help make Knox County more pet-friendly. In return, Ragsdale asked Boyd to help him form Knox Achieves, a scholarship program modeled after the Kalamazoo Promise. The Knox County version was funded by a mix of public and private dollars, and Boyd became a major donor to, and Board Chairman of, the effort. Also joining the board was the Mayor of the City of Knoxville, Bill Haslam. The program instantly showed signs of success in increasing student enrollment in their community and technical colleges, and it was expanded to twenty counties across Tennessee. By 2013, 40 percent of the state's high school graduates had access to the program.[98]

---

98 Gibson, M., *Who is Randy Boyd? Knoxville's Least-known Animal-loving Multi-Millionaire*

In 2014, Mayor Bill Haslam, a Republican, was elected Governor of Tennessee and, along with his newly-appointed Commissioner of Economic and Community Development, Randy Boyd, convinced the state's conservative legislature to take the idea statewide. Renamed the Tennessee Promise, it made all the state's community colleges tuition-free for qualifying high school graduates. It became the centerpiece of Governor Haslam's efforts to improve the skills of the state's workforce.

That effort caught the attention of President Obama, who traveled to Tennessee in January of 2015 to join Governor Haslam at a bipartisan event to announce the President's proposal for an initiative, not coincidentally named America's College Promise, to make all the country's community colleges free. Even though that idea ran into partisan gridlock in Congress, momentum for making college tuition free has continued to build at both the community and state level ever since.

Within a year of the Tennessee Republican legislature enacting the program, the Democratic legislature in Oregon adopted a similar one. The next year, six other states of different partisan persuasions made their community colleges free, with New York upping the ante by making its four-year colleges and universities tuition-free as well. Some of that growth occurred, as Rogers' theory said it should, through competition with neighboring states. Kentucky and Arkansas, for example, adopted Promise Programs, which, while smaller in scope, were their way of responding to the popularity of Tennessee's program, not just among voters, but with employers as well. Other states, such as Rhode Island and Nevada, simply emulated that which was already proving successful in Tennessee in order to meet their own workforce development needs. But none of it would have happened without the initial efforts of private citizens demonstrating the value of the idea to the future governor of Tennessee.[99]

Given the civic crisis of our time, we cannot leave the spread of local innovations to such serendipitous events. Currently, the mechanisms for spreading knowledge about what is working in cities and counties across regions, or even within a state, are too weak to fully guarantee the spread of good ideas across the country. We need a new way of rapidly and effec-

---

Business Magnate Philanthropist, Knoxville Mercury, April 1, 2015

99 Two of the authors of this book serve as President and Vice-President of the Campaign for Free College Tuition and have been personally involved in these state initiatives.

tively sharing ideas that work at the local level with other communities and up the policy communication channels within every state. The original idea of having the states be the laboratories of democracy posited that such policy experiments would then serve to inform the adoption of a national policy on the same issue, using a network of politicians as the social system for public policy innovation. However, Constitutional Localism inserts a new lower level into this social system by focusing on individual communities where we believe such innovation is more likely to occur with greater public support. As a result, without a way to strengthen this part of the country's public policy social system, Constitutional Localism risks adding additional delays to the spread of good ideas, an unacceptable outcome given the urgent need to improve the functioning of American democracy.

To avoid that result, a new "social system," as Rogers uses the term, for sharing and reproducing innovative ideas that have proven effective at the local level must be put in place, enabled by the enhanced capabilities of to-day's communication systems. The country must build such a social system, which we call SHARE, to SHare, Assess and REplicate innovative community ideas that will be as distinctive and innovative as the alphabet soup of federal agencies Franklin Delano Roosevelt put in place to implement the New Deal.

CONNECTING COMMUNITIES BY SHARING WHAT WORKS

New networks of local governing organizations must be put in place at the regional, state, or even federal level, using big data and predictive analytics, combined with the power of social media platforms. The networks will serve a twofold purpose— sharing and reviewing the results of local gov-ernmental efforts and encouraging the replication of those that are working through market incentives or properly-structured legislation. We believe the establishment and use of SHARE networks will be a major element in ulti-mately determining the success of Constitutional Localism by addressing the challenges facing the country and transforming America's governing bodies from an obstacle to overcome to a key source for solutions.

SHARE networks connecting the nation's communities would seek to replace an informal process of idea transfer with a more systematic one. It would build off the proven success of analogous efforts, often termed "PerformanceStats," that government leaders have used to improve results ever since this innovation was first implemented in New York City by Police

Commissioner Bill Bratton, in 1994. He called his crime fighting approach, COMPSTAT, and it gained wide-spread popularity when it produced a 77% reduction in crime in New York city, with homicides dropping to the lowest levels since reliable records were first created in 1963. The city had 75% fewer robberies in 2006 than it had in 1990, with essentially the same population, schools, and transportation system. The turnaround was so central to the revival of city life in all five boroughs that the most liberal mayor in recent New York history, Bill DeBlasio, brought Bratton back, along with his management approach, as the first appointee of his new administration.

Martin O'Malley, then mayor of Baltimore, expanded this local innovation to city functions other than policing. The television program, "The Wire," popularized the history of its implementation in fighting crime in that city, but the mayor went on to use the same approach to make sure basketball hoops were in place in every city park and garbage was picked up on time in every alley. He then used the popularity of the new level of city-government effectiveness as a springboard to the Maryland governor's office, where he championed the concept to improve the performance of state government.

After Hurricane Katrina, New Orleans mayor, Mitch Landrieu, launched BlightSTAT to "monitor progress on meeting citywide blight goals" and "help identify what works, what doesn't, and what needs to change in order for the City to meet its goals." BlightStat meetings were held each month in city hall and were open to the public, allowing citizens to ask questions and offer suggestions on how to improve blight-reduction programs. By July 2012, after 35 BlightSTAT meetings, the city had removed 4,500 blighted units. In 2013, the city met its blight reduction goal.[100]

In Los Angeles County, the STATS process of sharing, assessing, and replicating good ideas was used successfully to transfer the powerful problem-solving process from one agency to another as an intra-governmental tool. Taking the fundamental principles of "PerformanceStats", the county encouraged department heads to use the approach, which it called simply "STATS", to solve a multitude of service delivery challenges. The L.A. County Department of Public Social Services (DPSS), which administers the largest delivery of welfare services in the country, used it to improve client satisfaction with their interactions with the agency, as well as to improve the accuracy of the DPSS determination of eligibility for food stamps. The L.A. County

---

100 *PerformanceStat*, Evidence-Based Policymaking Collaborative, September 11, 2016

Mental Health Department also used STATS to ensure that clients were appropriately served, in addition to making certain that the county was properly reimbursed by the state for doing so. Another STATS implementation made it more difficult for dead-beat dads in the county to avoid making child-support payments. Each county agency learned from its peers, improving the process and their own results, as they went along.

Today, large cities across the country are using similar information-sharing processes to improve their services by taking advantage of computing technologies not available to STATS pioneers. As the book, *The Responsive City,* documents, cities leading this effort, such as New York, Boston, and Chicago, have combined the power of big data and data analytics with the reach and currency of social media. Now, residents in these cities can snap a picture of a pot hole, for example, text it to city bureaucrats from a smart phone, and ensure that the problem has been addressed, by tracking the process in real time. Such personalized, individual engagement enables thousands of city residents to experience daily the efficacy of democratic government organizations, and to share that experience with their skeptical friends, healing American democracy one pot hole at a time.[101]

Social media make information-sharing, assessment, and replication faster, better, and cheaper, thus enabling a more rapid spread of the process. Such technologies provide the perfect platforms for sharing information at practically no cost, enabling "ridiculously easy group formation." As Clay Shirky points out, "by lowering transaction costs, social tools provide a platform for "communities of practice," which are a much more efficient way of filtering out the good from the bad than traditional, more hierarchical systems.[102]

Technological advances and easier access to data are not sufficient, however, to assure the spread and effectiveness of SHARE networks on the scale and at the speed needed to address our current crisis in democratic confidence. More formal and consistent actions are also required. As Bob Behn, the guru of "PerformanceStats," points out, "Public and nonprofit agencies will certainly benefit from the insights produced by data wonks [in PerformanceStats meetings]. But to get real humans to act on these insights

101 Goldsmith, S. and Crawford, S. *The Responsive City,* Wiley Bass, 2014

102 *Shirky, C., Here Comes Everybody: The Power of Organizing Without Organizations,* Penguin Books, 2009

requires effective leadership."[103]

MAKING CONSTITUTIONAL LOCALISM HAPPEN

We believe governors may be in the best position to provide this leadership because of their existing relationships with mayors in their states, but recent events in some states suggest that governors may also bring unwelcome ideological bias to such discussions. This would undercut the central premise of SHARE exchanges, which, in order to be successful, require the objective search for what works, uncolored by personal or partisan agendas.

If governors aren't willing or able to exercise such leadership, SHARE networks could be built by voluntary associations of mayors or other elected officials, based on existing structures such groups have for sharing best practices. Former New York Mayor Michael Bloomberg has launched a $200 million "American Cities Initiative," in partnership with the U.S. Conference of Mayors. Its focus on empowering mayors and city governments to innovate and solve problems could be used to build these networks within this existing social system.[104] However, building SHARE networks would require the leaders of the Conference, or its subject- matter "councils," to engage their colleagues in something more than the typical "show and tell" exercises that often occur at conferences or conventions. Holding regular meetings with open discussion of data and outcomes, led by someone charged with initiating additional action to spread results on what works, would represent a radical change in the scope and authority of local elected-official associations. Just such a transformative shift will be required to accelerate our current civic efforts to increase community innovation and performance.

Where all this local policy momentum from the establishment and expansion of SHARE networks will lead is impossible to predict. It is also dangerous to try to determine in advance. For the country to once again demonstrate the power of democracy, we need to let a thousand local ideas bloom before deciding which ones should be replicated and which should not. In addition, different communities will develop different solutions to their challenges that may not meet the needs of other communities.

---

103 Behn, R.D., *Data Wonks and Performance Leaders,* April 8, 2015

104 *Michael R. Bloomberg Announces $200 Million American Cities Initiative to help U.S. Cities Innovate, Solve Problems, and Work Together in New Ways,* Bloomberg Philanthropies, June 26, 2017

We are not, therefore, putting forward a comprehensive list of new policy ideas designed to solve all the problems the country faces based upon our recommended new civic ethos of Constitutional Localism. Instead, we are proposing a new governance activity—SHARE— to ensure that ideas that work at the local level become known and propagated across the country, thereby building popular support for the idea of Constitutional Localism, as well. Because we believe that America's challenges can best be addressed by trusting in the imagination and creativity of local citizens to solve their own problems and, eventually, those of the country; we are advocating the creation of SHARE networks that connect local governments with their constituents and peers to make sure great ideas become known to all those equally committed to strengthening the functioning of our democracy.

We do not envision constitutional amendments or bold new statutes to accelerate the dominance of Constitutional Localism as the way America increasingly organizes governance in the twenty-first century. Instead, we favor a much more organic process to expand the role and responsibilities of local communities in our governing system.

The Great Recession delivered conclusive evidence that the federal partnership with cities instituted by the New Deal civic ethos was over, leaving cities no choice but to fend for themselves. Those localities fortunate enough to have the political leadership, social capital, and underlying economic resources to take advantage of the opportunity created by federal and, in some cases, state government's abdication of responsibility were able to seize the economic and social initiative for their communities on their own. As a result, some of the nation's largest metropolitan areas have emerged as the "engines of economic prosperity and social transformation in the United States."[105] As Bruce Katz and Jennifer Bradley wrote in *The Metropolitan Revolution*:

> Empowered by their economic strength and driven by demographic dynamism, cities and metros are positioning themselves at the cutting edge of reform, investment, and innovation. In traditional political science textbooks, the United States is portrayed neatly as a hierarchical structure—the federal government and the states on top, the cities and metropolitan areas at the bottom.... The metropolitan revolution is exploding this tired construct. Cities and metropolitan areas are becoming the leaders in the nation: experimenting, taking risk, making hard choices, and asking forgiveness, not permission.

---

105 Katz, B and Bradley, J, *The Metropolitan Revolution*, Brookings Institution Press, 2013

Public opinion strongly supports communities as the preferred venue for wrestling with common problems. The successes of an increasing number of America's large cities in dealing with issues ranging from public education to crime control to economic development, will build even more support for Constitutional Localism. Beyond this inevitable growth, there are three concrete steps that should be taken to further accelerate this trend and embed Constitutional Localism in our civic culture.

First, local leaders must be encouraged to publicly proclaim their emerging role as the initiators of civic innovation. Associations of mayors, township supervisors, county elected officials, and other local authorities should embrace the status of their governing bodies as the new laboratories of democracy. This will further the expectation that local communities are where many of the problems America faces will be effectively confronted and solved. Power is never willingly given up. If communities are to play an expanded role in the governance of our democracy, their leaders will have to assert their new role and responsibility.

Second, these same local government officials, perhaps with the leadership of state governors, will have to adopt the "smart city" approach that the Ash Center is promoting and proactively create SHARE networks to permit the more rapid sharing of local ideas that work. As a major practitioner of such management practices when he was mayor of New York, Michael Bloomberg's financial support and management expertise in partnership with the U.S. Conference of Mayors could provide just the spark SHARE networks need to make them a reality. Encouragingly, he said he launched this initiative in response to "an enormous demand" from mayors for just such a network.[106] Relying solely on the serendipitous spread of successful public solutions to communities with similar challenges and up the ladder to state and federal decision makers is not a viable strategy, given the urgency of the country's current needs.

Third, citizens outside of government who care about their local communities must dramatically increase their participation in local civic and political activities. After all, citizen participation is a critical measure of democratic health. One early cause should be repealing existing state laws that preempt local initiatives and helping state legislatures resist the temptation to enact new ones.

---

106 Lee, K., *A Helping Hand for Cities,* Los Angeles Times, July 28, 2017

Constitutional Localism is, by definition, a bottom-up movement. Without strong citizen advocacy, it is not likely to work, especially in the face of opposition from entrenched political interests that have a stake in the current status quo of gridlock and division. Our nation's history suggests Constitutional Localism will ultimately overcome these political obstacles if enough dedicated citizens get involved in its creation.

CHAPTER SEVEN:
CONSTITUTIONAL LOCALISM IS THE SOLUTION TO A UNIQUELY AMERICAN CHALLENGE

The idea of a new civic ethos, Constitutional Localism, fits well within the framework of American democracy and our history of regularly updating our democratic order to reflect evolving cultural and economic realities. America's Founders launched the nation with a predisposition to put self-governing as close to the people as circumstances permitted. Each successive civic ethos this country has adopted reflected the struggle to define the right balance between centralized and distributed governing authority and the rights of citizens that best met the challenges of its day. Now we need to put in place a fourth civic ethos that does just that in these troubled times.

Our belief that Constitutional Localism is the wave of the future is based, in part, on its inherent popularity. As discussed earlier, a substantial majority of Americans trust local government more than federal, or even state government, to reflect their interests and solve their problems. In addition, a growing number of cities and metropolitan areas are taking advantage of this strong public support for more local decision-making amid the paralysis in Washington, D. C. and many state capitols. They are not waiting for federal and state permission to seize the initiative to serve as the nation's new laboratories of democracy and are already taking actions that Constitutional Localism would further encourage.

In the 1930s and beyond, the New Deal civic ethos altered American federalism by including localities as "third partners" in the federal system, resulting in large amounts of federal aid and active involvement by the federal government in cities' policies. However, as many of those programs lost popular support in the 1970s and 1980s, the money and the collaboration with the federal government dried up. Left to sink or swim, with a growing number of implementation tasks imposed on them by both federal and state officials, but with dwindling revenue sources, many cities struggled to find the money to effectively dispatch their new-found responsibilities.[107]

The Great Recession delivered conclusive evidence that the federal partnership with cities instituted by the New Deal civic ethos was over, leaving the cities no choice but to fend for themselves. Those localities fortunate enough to have the political leadership, social capital, and underlying economic resources to take advantage of the opportunity created by the federal government's abdication of responsibility were able to seize the economic and social initiative for their communities

However, not all localities are participating in this explosion of economic innovation and social invention. Many smaller towns, exurbs, and rural areas with fewer resources to respond to the challenge have continued to struggle since the Great Recession, resulting in their young people moving to more urban areas and their economic anchors closing or pulling up stakes. The result has been increased feelings of being "left behind" and "disrespected" and the emergence of social ills, such as crime and opioid addiction, that were previously the types of scourges people moved to small towns to avoid. It has also left many small-town and rural citizens feeling politically alienated and questioning the efficacy of democratic processes.

The promise of greater local authority and resources proposed by Constitutional Localism provides the women and men of these communities with the tools to try to build new futures without having to wait passively for federal and state officials they don't trust to either care about their fate or to find effective solutions to their problems. Those Americans who express a strong desire to continue to live in the communities in which they grew up and raised their children and who want the locality they love to become successful again have two choices: they can either wait to be rescued by proposals from federal and state public officials, or they can be empowered to define a new future for themselves by choosing or embracing a new civic ethos—Constitutional Localism.

Despite growing evidence that Americans are encouraging more activism on the part of their local community, fundamental shifts in governing paradigms have always been difficult to manage. In the past, each new civic compact emerged only after an exhaustive and acrimonious debate in a context of widespread frustration, anger, and bitter, partisan division. In each

---

107 Riverstone-Newell, Lori, *Renegade Cities, Public Policy, and the Dilemmas of Federalism,* First Forum Press, 2014

instance, a broad, but by no means unanimous, agreement was forged about how best to assign responsibility for achieving that new understanding of national direction among the various levels of government and their citizens. Historically, the debate over a new civic ethos ultimately led to an electoral triumph by the political party that seized the opportunity to make the new civic framework its brand, but not until after a full and robust national discussion (lethal in 1860) about which direction the nation should take.

As the evidence provided in this book makes clear, we are again in such a period. In the short term, we need to find venues and processes whereby Americans can escape polarization and gridlock and collectively solve problems that are impeding progress and injuring families' well-being. In the longer run, we must reestablish faith in our basic democratic values as the only way to secure an American identity. It is the only path forward, based on freedom and self-government, that will enable the United States to flourish as one nation, given its broad diversity of cultural preferences and economic interests—a degree of diversity we have never before experienced in our nation's history. It is time for America to agree on a new civic ethos that reflects a consensus on the scope and purpose of government in order to save our democracy and enable the country to succeed in the twenty-first century.

The challenge is considerable. America is more divided now than it has been at any time since the Civil War. Political differences influence our decisions about where we live, who our friends are, and even what foods we eat. More ominously, these divisions have prevented the building of the broad national majorities needed to solve pressing problems confronting American families, such as wage stagnation, income inequality, health care access and cost, threats from climate change, racial conflict, declining upward mobility, and finding our place in a rapidly-changing and dangerous world. The list is long, and no one solution will solve all of the country's problems. But withdrawing from the arena in despair over the size of the challenge is not the American way. Instead, we need to take the first steps to address the problem and channel America's fondness for local activism and civic engagement into a national effort that will find solutions to our problems one community and one problem at a time.

Millennials are the generation most likely to embrace the challenge and a bottom-up solution to address it. Older generations that came of age in the political context of today's civic ethos, are more likely to resist transformative change or insist any change start at the top of our governmental hierarchy. Fortunately for the country's future, Millennials will assume more and more power in the coming decades, bringing their suspicion of solutions dictated from on high into a prominent place in our civic dialogue. Their facility with social media will also provide an already-sophisticated group of users for participation in the type of "smart city" solutions that will be at the heart of SHARE networks. And their belief in working together to find consensus solutions is precisely the type of behavior that will make Constitutional Localism successful. And, even though Plurals, members of the generation that follows Millennials, are still too young to have registered their political preferences, it is already clear that their own experiences growing up in the most diverse American society ever, have inculcated these very same traits of inclusion and love of community in their approach to solving problems. Although these generational trends make the future of Constitutional Localism bright, the opposition to its adoption will be fierce in the near term.

Ironically, the deep political distrust that Constitutional Localism is designed to overcome may turn out to be the greatest obstacle to its adoption. Some on the Left will still see in its celebration of local decision-making the specter of state's rights and a backing away from civil rights and federal enforcement of anti-discrimination laws. Given the continuing separation of communities based on race or ethnicity, liberals might argue that Constitutional Localism is merely a cover for returning to the days of "Separate but Equal," that stained our nation's history for nearly a century. As early and passionate advocates for civil rights and integrated schools, we are particularly sensitive to such a critique; but we believe that by emphasizing the unbreakable boundary of constitutional rights in its implementation, Constitutional Localism can avoid this unacceptable outcome.

Some on the Right will see Constitutional Localism as a way for liberals to dilute the power to set national policy that conservatives theoretically now enjoy, given their control of all three branches of the federal government. Republicans will be particularly skeptical of Democrats suddenly advocating for more local control, after decades of attempting to centralize regulatory power in Washington. We believe the need to revitalize American democracy supersedes any concerns about short-term political advantage either side might be seeking to gain, but we understand why Republicans might be suspicious of the other side's motives. Their concern is best addressed by making sure the movement to implement Constitutional Localism is a bi-partisan one in both word and deed.

In addition, some on both sides of the political spectrum may argue that Constitutional Localism will reinforce current trends toward individuals retreating into their own physical and virtual worlds, populated only by those who think and believe as they do. We believe, however, that such tendencies to tribalism can be mitigated by encouraging localities and the individuals who live in them to join SHARE networks and to participate in discussions that demonstrate the common ground they have with each other. Then, the outcomes of those discussions can lead to interactions with other communities that are also searching for solutions to today's challenges.

Because Constitutional Localism accepts the variety of life styles, political views, cultural and ethnic diversity, and geographic preferences that currently characterize the nation as evidence of Americans' freedom to travel different paths, some may see it as an idea that would further divide our country into competing camps, rather than unify us. We believe that, instead, Constitutional Localism can provide new, successful democratic experiences that will fortify a common American identity, based on shared democratic values and help heal the bonds of citizenship that have been broken by the size, pace, and nature of the changes the country has experienced. The Founders struggled with the unprecedented challenge of designing democratic governance for what they believed would become a continental nation, vastly larger than the city states to which democracies had previously been restricted. Today, we face the unique and equally formidable task of how to redesign our system of democratic governance for a nation that is not only physically large and separated, but one that is more disparate racially, religiously, culturally, and economically than any on earth. It is a humbling, but necessary, undertaking.

We believe that, in a time of diverse beliefs and life styles and dramatic demographic changes, Constitutional Localism provides the right distribution of governing power and responsibility that will allow our nation to progress and protect our democratic ideals.

We three are Democrats by political affiliation, but we do not see Constitutional Localism as the province of either party. We hope we have succeeded in our attempt to avoid bringing any ideological baggage to this discussion, save our unyielding belief that Constitutional democracy, as America has sought to practice it since 1789, is the best form of governance for a people who wish to be free and determine their own future.

Our purpose in writing this book is to contribute something of value to the critical debate about how best to preserve the American democratic experiment, not only for today, but for generations of Americans to come. We hope that Millennial readers, in particular, will be motivated to sign up to participate in many civic activities, so they can bring their attitudes of inclusion and consensus to everyone else in the communities in which they live. But regardless of your age or generational affiliation, we encourage you to join us in this debate about how to form a more perfect union with the intensity and urgency the times demand.

ACKNOWLEDGEMENTS

This book represents our conclusions after a yearlong discussion among three fast friends about how to make American democracy work at a time of intense political, cultural and economic division. Although the ideas, thoughts, and words contained in this book are most certainly those of its three authors, as are any inadvertent errors, we appreciate the efforts of those who tried to help us think more clearly about the topic along the way.

We have benefited from the ideas and suggestions from many people who lent the value of their own expertise to our endeavor, such as Dudley Buffa, Pete Markiewicz, Alan Glassman, and Pete Plastrik. We are also grateful for the early editing assistance and thoughtful observations of an emerging young scholar, Luke Phillips, who helped us clarify our ideas within the broader traditions of American political philosophy and history.

Above all we want to recognize the support of Joel Kotkin, Executive Director of the Center for Opportunity Urbanism, who, over the past few years, has been unrelenting in urging us to explore the implications and possibilities of localism and then proved his sincerity by helping to expose our ideas among a wide variety of settings and people. Rochelle Moulton, who is so much more than just our publicist, has continued to provide invaluable advice on how to ensure our ideas are heard by the people who can do the most to make Constitutional Localism a reality.

We have made every effort to be rigorous in basing our work on empirical evidence rather than trendy opinions or comfortable assumptions. The aggregate data provided by the U.S. Census Bureau and the survey research of the Pew Research Center, America's preeminent and prolific public polling organization, have been especially valuable in allowing us to stay on this path.

Finally, any acknowledgement of the support and help we have had in writing this book, must end with fulsome praise for our wives, each of whom has devoted a lifetime to making us look good. So, indulge us while we conclude by making individual statements to the most important people in our lives.

From Mike Hais: "Reena, this book is being published in the 50th year of our marriage and I want to thank you for five decades filled with your love, laughter, wisdom, and beauty of both form and spirit, and support in all of my endeavors including my participation in the writing of this book."

From Doug Ross: "I wish to express my gratitude to my talented wife and loving partner, Karol, for her enthusiastic and generous gift of the time, space, and encouragement to participate in this project."

From Morley Winograd: "My wife Bobbie has managed to find reasons to stay married to me for over 50 years, even though this is the second book I have co-authored since promising her never to write another one or asking her to help copyedit my writings. Thank you for being so tolerant and understanding of my faults and foibles for almost sixty years."